PUBLIC AGENCY COMMUNICATION

PUBLIC AGENCY COMMUNICATION
Theory and Practice

Hindy Lauer Schachter

New Jersey Institute of Technology

Nelson-Hall nh Chicago

Library of Congress Cataloging in Publication Data

Schachter, Hindy Lauer.
   Public agency communication.

   Includes index.
   1. Communication in public administration.
I. Title.
JF1525.C59S3   1983   350'.007   82-14144
ISBN 0-88229-742-2

Manufactured in the United States of America

10   9   8   7   6   5   4   3   2   1

The paper in this book is pH neutral (acid-free).

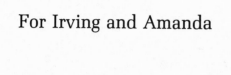

For Irving and Amanda

CONTENTS

PREFACE

No ability is as important to the public manager as the ability to speak and write effectively. Public administrators spend a good part of their work day speaking and listening, writing and reading; without the ability to impart and receive ideas, they cannot function effectively.

The aim of this book is to provide realistic knowledge on the exchange of information in local, state, and federal agencies. In four units, this handbook explores the theory and practice of intra-agency communication.

The first two units supply a background on communicating in agencies. Unit I defines the concept of communication and analyzes the importance of various channels and their relationship to decision making. The first chapter explores how agencies set up and maintain *formal* channels of communication, why *informal* channels spring up, and their role in spreading information. Subsequent chapters consider whether a vigorous *grapevine* is "good" or "bad" for an agency and how public administrators can use informal channels to help achieve the agency's goals.

The second unit identifies five common barriers to effective communication and explores individual and organizational strategies for minimizing them. These barriers are inappropriate language, status differences between the communicator and the audience, different frames of reference held by the communicator and the audience, geographical distance between agency units, and the pressure of other activities (e.g., time constraints).

The third and fourth units are practical how-to guides for developing and presenting effective intra-agency communications. Both units contain practice-oriented rules, examples from actual agency documents, and extensive exercises.

In Unit III, four types of oral communications are analyzed: how to give job instructions, conduct interviews, handle grievances, and chair staff meetings. Emphasis is placed on tailoring the style and content to the particular purpose of and audience for each presentation.

Preparing written documents is the focus of the last unit. Students develop the ability to collect and structure information and present it in a clear, well-organized manner. The emphasis is on writing effective memoranda, summaries, options and position papers, progress reports, and training manuals. An extensive section deals with the preparation of tables, charts, graphs, and statistical maps.

In preparing a book, an author always runs up debts. I want to thank Roy B. Helfgott, Chairman of the Department of Organizational and Social Sciences at New Jersey Institute of Technology, for encouragement, advice, and the released time that enabled me to complete this project. In addition, I want to take this opportunity to thank Donna E. Shalala, president of Hunter College, CUNY, who started me on my professional career; I owe her a great debt which I can never repay but which it is always a pleasure to acknowledge. Sherry Stansbury read the book in manuscript and made a number of helpful comments.

UNIT ONE

The Communication Process

1

Setting Up and Maintaining Agency Communications

It is a clear October day in Washington, D.C. At the National Institute of Health, a woman approves a grant to finance hospital construction in Indiana. Some blocks away, an analyst in the Department of Defense addresses a staff meeting on purchase estimates for new weapons and delivery systems. Outside a window, a fire captain shouts orders to a crew dousing a three-alarm blaze. A police officer chats nonchalantly with a buddy about the cruel new sergeant who gave them such a rough time.

What do the grants administrator, the defense analyst, the fire captain, and the police officer have in common? They are all public administrators engaged in communication.

Communication, or conveying information, is the lifeblood of public agencies. It is the most consistent activity in all public organizations, touching all departments and affecting everybody from the agency head to the clerks and janitors. It involves every conceivable communication technique including (but certainly not limited to) books, pamphlets, reports, telephone conversations, informal chats, and a whole repertoire of gestures.

Suppose someone asked you: "What does a public agency need in order to function?" Your first answer might be money. Another answer might be people. It is impossible for any organization to function without these resources (that is why public administration curricula usually include a course in budgeting and one in personnel administration).

However, an agency cannot function solely on money and people. The concept of organization presupposes the coming together of people to perform interdependent activities in order to move towards a common goal. Organization implies cooperation. It requires constant attempts at the transmission of intentions, knowledge, and experience from person to person. As psychologists Alex Bavelas and D. Barrett note:

> Communication is not a secondary . . . aspect of organizations—a "helper" of the other and more basic functions. Rather it is . . . the basic process out of which all other functions derive.[1]

An agency where administrators do not attempt to convey information can be compared to an air conditioner with the plug out; its use is only potential. Communication is the current that makes an agency move. The type of communication an agency gets determines how well it can perform its functions. Effective communication is indispensable for effective performance. Breakdowns in communication inevitably lead to agency problems.

This book explores strategies for communicating effectively in public agencies. However, before we discuss how to communicate, we must have a clear idea of what is meant by the words *communication* and *communication process*. We also need to understand the nature of administrative organizations in the public sector: why they are created, how they are structured, and what tasks they perform. Then we can discuss the purpose of communication in public agencies and the appropriate channels for transmitting various kinds of information.

WHAT IS COMMUNICATION?

Communication is the process of transmitting intentions, desires, feelings, knowledge, and experience among individuals.[2] It is a process of sharing information through which an idea or attitude passes from one person to another.

Figure 1.1 shows that communication always involves three elements: a communicator, a message, and an audience. Communicators function as the source of information.[3] They have messages—thoughts in their heads—that they want to share. Messages consist of the information itself and the channel through which this information is transmitted. A message may be sent in the form of ink on paper, sound waves in the air, a nod of the head, or any other signal that people can interpret. The communicator's first decision revolves around what signal to send.

For example, let us assume a police captain discovers that officers "coop" or sleep in a garage at night instead of patrolling their beats. The captain decides to let the officers know that he will not stand for such fooling around. His first concern is how to express his displeasure. Should he speak to each officer individually? Call a staff meeting? Write a memorandum? And what words should he use? Is it best to accuse the officers outright or to speak in generalities? How much stress should be put on punishment, how much on the public's need for constant protection?

These decisions are crucial. The way the captain encodes the message determines, to a large extent, how the officers decode or interpret it. Once coded and sent, a message is quite free of its sender; its effects can be beyond the power of the communicator to change. Filtering or distortion can take place when the audience decodes, thus creating a potential gap between the sender's intentions and the message the audience actually receives.

FORMAL COMMUNICATION CHANNELS

Every agency has a planned arrangement for transmitting information to those who need it. Those channels which are

FIG. 1.1. A MODEL OF THE COMMUNICATION PROCESS

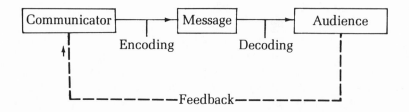

deliberately created by the legislature or top agency management constitute the *formal* communication channels; all other channels are *informal*.

Creating Formal Channels

Public agencies are organizations within the executive branch of federal, state, or local government concerned with the implementation of public programs. Legislatures create agencies in response to a demand for service or alleviation of problems that the public sees as a legitimate governmental concern. The Congress, or state or local legislature assigns each agency an overall goal or mission which, in turn, becomes its principle of organization. (For example, the goal of a fire department is to protect life and property from fire; the goal of a sanitation agency is to maintain a clean and healthy environment.)

In order to achieve its goal, every agency needs a means of transmitting information. The legislature that establishes an agency also sets up the basic framework for its internal communication. A line or two in the enabling legislation tells the agency's director to prescribe regulations or administrative procedures for the staff.

The legislature's mandate, however, is always too short to do more than outline how information will be exchanged. Top agency managers amplify and clarify the enabling legislation. Through regulations and guidelines they establish how internal orders, directives, and rules get initiated and transmitted. They specify who writes to whom, who receives various types of reports and memoranda, and how papers are routed. They establish a formal system for transmitting messages that the agency explicitly recognizes as official.

Formal communications tend to be written. The documents serve as official records of agency decisions. They have a semipermanent status; they are Xeroxed, filed, and theoretically kept available to be read and reread whenever an employee needs them.

As written messages, formal communications maintain behavioral uniformity. They restrain individual administrators from acting arbitrarily. Administrators know their actions can be evaluated against written directives that explain how top management wants employees to act.

Formal Channels and Agency Structure

Formal channels of communication generally coincide with an agency's structure or design. The most common structure among public organizations is the pyramid or hierarchy. One person on top has the legal right to make decisions for subordinates who, in turn, have the authority to command the next layer.

Administrators exercise authority by conveying information to their subordinates. Orders must be issued and transmitted if they are to have any chance of being obeyed. A constant stream of directives and reports indicating compliance moves up and down the hierarchy between superiors and subordinates.

Figure 1.2 shows the hierarchy or chain of command for the St. Louis Police Department. The vertical lines indicate who has the legal right to issue commands to whom; the flow of formal communications follows these lines of authority. For example, the chief of police (PC) has the authority to convey orders to and require compliance reports from the chief of field operations who, in turn, can issue orders to the commanders of Areas I through III and the commander of special operations. The commander of Area I, in turn, can transmit orders and prescribe compliance reports from subordinate officers in the first three districts.

The formal communication system makes no provision for direct communication between individuals who work in different

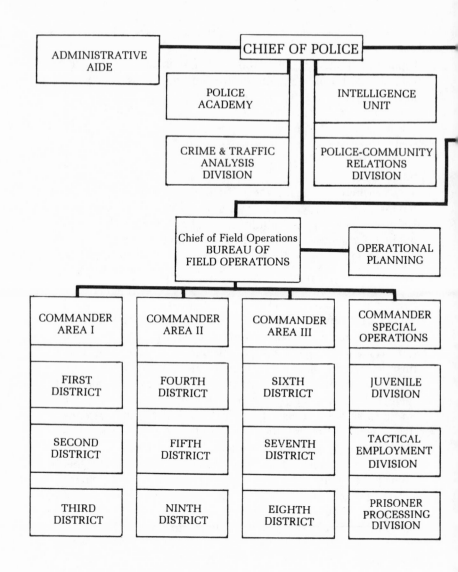

FIG. 1.2. ORGANIZATION CHART, METROPOLITAN POLICE DEPARTMENT, CITY OF ST. LOUIS.

Source: St. Louis Metropolitan Police Department, *Annual Report* (July 1974), p. 21.

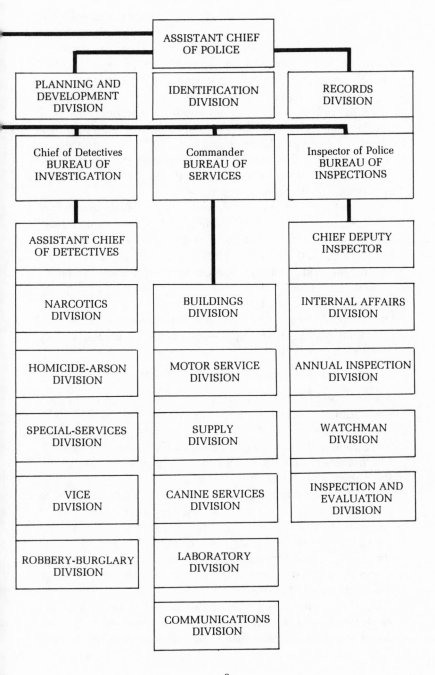

ASSISTANT CHIEF
OF POLICE

PLANNING AND
DEVELOPMENT
DIVISION

IDENTIFICATION
DIVISION

RECORDS
DIVISION

Chief of Detectives
BUREAU OF
INVESTIGATION

Commander
BUREAU OF
SERVICES

Inspector of Police
BUREAU OF
INSPECTIONS

ASSISTANT CHIEF
OF DETECTIVES

CHIEF DEPUTY
INSPECTOR

NARCOTICS
DIVISION

BUILDINGS
DIVISION

INTERNAL AFFAIRS
DIVISION

HOMICIDE-ARSON
DIVISION

MOTOR SERVICE
DIVISION

ANNUAL INSPECTION
DIVISION

SPECIAL-SERVICES
DIVISION

SUPPLY
DIVISION

WATCHMAN
DIVISION

VICE
DIVISION

CANINE SERVICES
DIVISION

INSPECTION AND
EVALUATION
DIVISION

ROBBERY-BURGLARY
DIVISION

LABORATORY
DIVISION

COMMUNICATIONS
DIVISION

9

units. In classical management theory, they must communicate formally through their division heads. For example, if the chief of field operations wants to communicate with the Narcotics Division, the message is routed up to the chief of police and then through the offices of the chief and assistant chief of detectives.

The central objective of this roundabout information routing is to avoid having an administrator receive conflicting orders on the same subject. But the process is often so long and complicated that agencies always supplement formal systems with other, less cumbersome, communication channels.

In general, the higher people's rank, the greater the number of formal communications they initiate and receive. Entry-level administrators get memoranda from immediate superiors. The Chief of Police receives memoranda from political officials such as the mayor, and from the Assistant Chief of Police, the Police Academy, the Intelligence Unit, the Crime and Traffic and Community Relations Divisions, and many other subordinates. Higher officials need a broader range of information because their authority has greater scope—they control a greater variety of persons and activities.

Formal Channels and Decision Making

Agencies set up formal channels of communication to transmit to each administrator the information needed in order to make decisions. Decision making is the process whereby administrators choose one course of action from available alternatives. All public managers make decisions, although they vary greatly in scope, range, and importance.

Let's say an agency's commissioner has to decide whether to start an affirmative action program. A subordinate, the director of personnel, must choose among alternative strategies for maximizing bias-free hiring. A testing and measurement specialist has to decide which selection examinations are usable. A personnel assistant chooses the wording for the agency's first recruitment ad in *El Diario*.

All these decision makers depend on different information for their different choices. The commissioner needs data on the political, social, and legal consequences of starting an affirmative action program. The director of personnel needs cost/benefit analyses of alternative affirmative action strategies. The testing and measurement specialist wants descriptions of bias-free examinations. The personnel assistant seeks information on *El Diario*'s requirements for recruitment ads.

It is rare for administrators to hold in their hands all the information they need to make a particular decision. Sometimes they have to consult subordinates. Sometimes they seek data from staff members who work in specialized departments. (For example, both the commissioner and the personnel director might seek information from the agency's legal bureau.) Sometimes they must obtain information from outside, for example, *El Diario*'s current requirements.

Ideally, each decision maker gets exactly the information needed—no less and no more. In actuality, however, this neat fit rarely (if ever) occurs. It is often impossible to tell in advance what information each staff member will need. Since formal channels are created long before most agency decisions are made, they frequently carry too little data to the decision maker or too much data in the form of duplications, overlaps, and inclusion of frivolous materials. The challenge to the designer of a communication system is to create one that carries sufficient information to each decision maker without generating useless information—pages and pages that lie unread.

Communication and Centralization

Who should make a particular decision? This question often sparks intense debate in public agencies. Should principals alone have the authority to suspend unruly pupils or should the right be given to individual teachers? Should the directors of social service centers have to certify applications for income assistance or can the decision be made by the caseworkers?

A key factor in locating a *decision center* is to determine the most accessible lines of information available to the decision maker.[4] Will the principal have better information about the pupil than the teacher? Does the director have more accurate data on certifying applications or does the caseworker? If the superior has access to better information, then the agency gains by centralizing decision making. If the subordinate has easier access, then there are rewards to decentralization.

To complicate matters, each level of the hierarchy generally has easier access to certain kinds of information. Thus both centralizing and decentralizing have their own benefits and costs.

Top administrators have a better picture of the agency's overall strategies and how particular actions help to attain broad goals. Centralized decision making increases uniformity, the probability that all decisions are consistent.

Subordinates tend to have more information on the details of cases they are working on. They have first-hand knowledge about particular clients. Teachers have daily contact with unruly pupils while principals rarely enter classrooms. Caseworkers interview welfare applicants; their supervisors learn about the clients from reports written by the caseworkers. Decisions made by entry-level administrators take into account more of the details that make any encounter with human beings unique. They tend to be more flexible and responsive than decisions made at the apex of the hierarchy.

The public expects both consistency and flexibility. Equity demands that administrators treat similar cases in a uniform manner. Sensitivity to the varied needs of communities and individuals leads bureaucrats to treat cases on their individual merits when such cases "by common human standards of justice or benevolence, seem to require that an exception be made or a rule stretched."[5]

Ultimately each agency must examine its own mission and values and select the degree of centralization that fits its goals. Thus, the Treasury Department centralizes decision making for internal revenue agents because the public demands a consistent policy on tax law. During the 1960s, several big cities decentralized educational decision making in order to increase each school's responsiveness to its own community.

INFORMAL COMMUNICATION CHANNELS

Agencies always supplement their formal communication systems with a great deal of spontaneous information exchange.

No matter how elaborately the formal systems are planned, employees always find opportunities for sharing information through unauthorized channels—even through those that are expressly forbidden.

For two reasons, the formal system can never supply all of the data that administrators need. First, the formal system follows the chain of command; thus it fails to provide channels for communicating horizontally, i.e., between equals or peers.

Look again at figure 1.2. Formal channels exist for the chief of detectives to transmit orders to subordinates (e.g., the assistant chief). However, formal channels do not indicate how to communicate directly with peers such as the commander of the Bureau of Services and the head of the Bureau of Inspections. In order to solve a case, the chief might want to exchange data directly with an equal. This necessary but unplanned communication takes place outside the formal system.

Another problem with the formal structure is that it uses written channels, and they are notoriously slow. Reports and memoranda often transmit information after it is needed. (Imagine waiting for a memorandum to find out that the office is on fire!)

In order to get the information they need, administrators fill in the gaps left by the "official" system. Informal channels are born when peers engage in unplanned "shop talk" or superiors and subordinates have off-the-record conversations.

Both formal and informal systems are important to the agency. They differ in their origin (planned versus unplanned) rather than in their worth. Messages sent in either system run the gamut from vital to petty.

Many important agency decisions are actually based on information communicated informally. After the choice is made, a written message legitimizes it. For example, a bureau chief holds off-the-record conversations with assistants before dividing work assignments. Since the talks are informal, the assistants can easily withdraw or alter their preferences. After the group reaches a consensus, the bureau chief sends a memorandum outlining responsibilities.

Over time, certain informal procedures work so well that they achieve a "semiformal" status. For example, young nurses in a certain public health clinic always turn to an older colleague when they need advice. The older nurse has no formal authority over training, but new recruits quickly learn that he is a more up-to-date source than the official manual.

Growth of Informal Channels

Informal channels are particularly strong when:

1. Bureau members have stable relations with each other. (The staff is not constantly changing.)

2. The bureau's environment is uncertain. (Gossip and rumor thrive when the environment changes. Administrators are in doubt about what will happen next and consult the "grapevine" for the latest news.)

3. The bureau is operating under great time pressure. (During a crisis, informal channels assume a particularly important role. Top decision makers are desperate for usable information and reach out to whoever seems to have it. They tend to rely on staff members with whom they have personal relationships even if these people have no formal responsibility in the crisis area.)[6]

Face-to-Face Communication

One reason for the popularity of informal systems is that they allow more personal channels of exchange. Research indicates that face-to-face communication is a particularly effective way of transmitting information because[7]:

1. Oral communication to one individual or small groups permits greater flexibility. (The communicator gets instant *feedback* or return on how the audience receives the message. When you talk to less than ten people, you tend to know whether you are getting your point across. The listeners nod their heads, say "Yes, you're right," or frown perplexedly. If you see that the message does not travel, you repeat phrases or try a different tack. You try to tailor the message to the particular needs of each member of a small audience; you explain and re-explain what you really mean.)

2. Personal contacts are difficult to avoid. (It is relatively easy to shunt an unpleasant memorandum or leave a manual unread.

Administrators are less likely to shove colleagues out of their offices or stop them in mid-sentence.)

3. Conversations are exercises in friendship as well as information exchange. (Informal communications place an emphasis on the agency staff as individuals and not as holders of official roles. Administrators enter into them in order to enhance personal as well as organizational goals. Officials accept oral requests from colleagues simply because they want to have pleasant relations with them, not necessarily because they agree with the content of the messages.)

Face-to-Face and Formal Communication

The importance of oral channels extends to helping formal communications reach agency members. Shop talk plays a role in spreading the contents of written orders.

Every public administrator belongs to an informal communication network composed of friends and peers. These networks discuss new directives when they are issued; the opinions of each member influence the attitudes of the others. Conversations at desk, water cooler, or lunchroom table affect how given agency employees interpret a memo from the boss and the extent to which they modify behavior in response to a hierarchical command.

Informal group attitudes have a major impact on the way staff accept formal communications. Their effect can be positive or negative, enhancing or detracting from productivity. In either case, it is important for high-level administrators to understand group dynamics and how informal patterns influence an agency's ability to reach its goal.

2

Communication and Informal Groups

The preceding chapter described how well-knit informal groups affect agency communication. Now we delve more deeply into group dynamics and the influence social bonds have on goal-directed information exchange. We begin by analyzing why groups form—the factors that prompt administrators to seek on-the-job companionship and social contact.

WHY GROUPS FORM

Administrators join groups because they satisfy the need for friendship, assistance, and protection.

Friendship

Public agencies are much too large for the organization itself to serve as a friendship group. The masses of administrators at the bottom and middle ranks are anonymous to their superiors and their colleagues who work in other departments.

The only unit that can provide a sense of community and

companionship is the small group that consists of the administrators who interact with each other face-to-face offering *Gemeinschaft* or communal, as opposed to *Gesellschaft* or formal, segmented relations. When the daily work routine abounds with tension, informal chats are a mechanism for discharging venom and receiving personalized understanding.

Assistance

Groups provide work-related assistance to their members. One study finds that administrators consistently prefer asking friends rather than managers for aid in solving complicated problems,[1] even when the bureau officially discourages peer communication. Friends "spell" each other in case of illness; they rotate unpleasant aspects of a job. They pass along shortcuts and effective ways to eliminate red tape.

A *cabal* is one type of group formed principally for its assistance function. Administrators with an intense desire to move up in the organization may form a cabal to help each other climb the agency's hierarchical ladder.[2] They pass along shortcuts and effective ways of coming to the attention of supervisors. But cabals are generally unstable; they break up when one or two members see an opportunity to rise by currying individual favor with the unit manager.

Protection

Groups also protect members from supervisory pressure. They cover up for inadvertent mistakes, get even with "squealers," and informally (but effectively) discipline administrators who refuse to aid co-workers.

A woman who processes grants at the federal Office of Economic Opportunity explains that one worker never gives the supervisor incriminating information about another: "If he'd want to find out what time someone come in, who's gonna tell 'em? . . . You know how the game is played. Tomorrow you might need a favor."[3]

A *clique* is one type of group formed principally for protection against supervisors. Created by older employees who have been bypassed for promotion, it can be very effective because members (with extensive seniority) know all the weak spots in their supervisor's armor.[4]

Groups also provide psychological protection from public attack. Individual administrators are often the target of criticism (justified or not) from clients or political officials who have to evaluate an agency's performance. When such an attack commences, the administrator's colleagues almost inevitably reassure him that outsiders cannot evaluate his actions because they do not understand the environment in which he performs.

Police groups are particularly prone to offer such protection. Accuse officers of using excessive force and their companions almost invariably rush to their defense stressing that outsiders cannot possibly comprehend the dangers inherent in police work and the need for split-second judgment. This pushbutton rush-to-defense makes some critics charge that modern administrators protect each other at the public's expense.

How Groups Operate

Once administrators establish informal groups, a dynamic linked-chain process begins. The interaction of agency members creates bonds of friendship and group loyalty. The rewards of companionship, in turn, lead to further interaction: colleagues synchronize lunch hours, coffee breaks, and off-the-job activities. Additional interactions yield even stronger loyalties, thus building a firm sense of group solidarity.[5]

Eventually the group develops an internal structure of its own which includes many of the characteristics of formal organizations—goals, leaders, rules, and procedures. It develops its own *norms* or standards of conduct. It acquires a unique way of doing things, a customary pattern of behavior that high authorities have difficulty changing (if they see the need to try).

Every administrator has to decide what his relationship will be to the dominant group or groups in his unit. He may choose from several roles:

1. a regular member, accepting and conforming to group norms;

2. a deviant, rejecting one or more norms but still interacting socially with other members;

3. an isolate, rejecting personal, informal contacts; or

4. a leader, having special (albeit informal) status.[6]

Groups develop ways to punish those who deviate from their norms. Ostracism, needling, and sarcasm can all be the lot of administrators who fail to help colleagues.

However, effective groups rarely punish. There is something wrong with an informal association that has to constantly apply sanctions just as there is something wrong with an agency that has to constantly fire employees. When informal groups function properly, members conform because the group's norms meet their own needs—not because they fear punishment. A group that constantly has to punish deviants is probably in danger of foundering or splitting apart.

Cohesion

Effective groups have *cohesion*, a high degree of attraction for their members. The more cohesive or unified a group, the more likely its members are to conform to its norms and act together against a perceived threat from the supervisor or another unit.

Five unit variables influence a group's cohesion: size, homogeneity, status, physical isolation, and pressure.[7] Let us examine each.

Size. Small units tend to have more cohesive groups than large ones. Administrators form groups through face-to-face contact so it is easier to have frequent chats with all members of a small unit.

Homogeneity. Friendship and identification grow more easily when personnel come from similar social and educational backgrounds. When all members of a unit share professional training, the probability of a cohesive work group is high. Administrators share assumptions and prior experiences which facilitates their interaction.

Status. Other things being equal, administrators are more likely to feel loyalty to high rather than low status groups. Climbers in an agency often disregard the norms of the group they belong to and embrace those of the group they want to join.

Physical isolation. Isolation of a group fosters cohesion. Nurses working the midnight to eight shift socialize almost exclusively with each other because their schedule isolates them from much contact with friends working from nine to five. American personnel in overseas missions entertain each other frequently; their isolation makes them so inbred that federal legislation requires a number of mid-career Foreign Service Officers to rotate their tours of duty.

Pressure.   Groups band together when they feel under attack from outside. One reason police officers in high-crime districts almost invariably have cohesive groups is that they see themselves as "sacrificial lambs,"[8] the targets of sharp criticism delivered by their "clients" and supervisors.

Split Groups

Some units never develop cohesive informal networks. For instance, there could be two or three groups in a given unit; each has high internal cohesion but its members view the other groups with some suspicion and distrust.

Split groups appear when unit personnel come from different backgrounds, as for example, when their educations or career paths vary. The State Department staffs some Washington bureaus with Foreign Service Officers (FSOs) and experts who are not members of the foreign service.[9] FSOs are selected on the basis of excellent general background, intelligence, and overall aptitude. Their "subculture" is rooted in their unique overseas responsibilities where the department places a premium on field experience and intuition as opposed to specialized academic training. Non-FSO experts are selected on the basis of their mastery of a particular policy specialization. They will spend their entire careers in Washington with their status largely based on academic credentials. Their subculture puts its premium on formal problem-solving approaches rather than field experience or gut intuition.

It should come as no surprise to discover that many experts stereotype FSOs as dilettantes. FSOs in turn condemn experts for being myopic, overspecialized, and incapable of seeing the forest for the trees.

When FSOs and experts work in the same unit, split groups develop. An outsider can tell who belongs to which by asking

administrators, "Where do you work?" Foreign policy experts
generally respond, "I work for the State Department." Officers
answer, "I'm an FSO." Split groups also develop when
previously segregated units hire their first black, Indian, Eskimo,
Mexican-American, female, or handicapped administrators. The
incumbents almost always accept the newcomers in their formal
roles but they may be unwilling to associate informally. Then two
or more groups emerge, one for majority males (the "old boy"
network) and the others for minorities and women.

Each group has its own communication network, its own gossip
and grapevine. Each spreads its own rumors—often about the
other. If supervisors cannot bring the groups together, intergroup
hostility and mistrust multiply, thus making it difficult for people
in either group to perform their formal tasks. There is even a
possibility of intergroup violence, particularly when the
employees live together, e.g., in a firehouse or on board a ship.

When the navy doubled the number of black sailors in the
early 1970s, integrating many vessels for the first time, two
informal groups—one white, one black—developed on many
ships. On the aircraft carrier U.S.S. *Constellation*, black and
white enlisted personnel each appropriated a different
barbershop as a gathering spot. These were fertile breeding
grounds for prejudice; a sailor could enter one, make derogatory
remarks about members of the other group, and have absolutely
no fear that any outsider would contradict him. Since the officers
did little to promote informal communication between groups,
mistrust grew. Eventually intergroup suspicion ignited into a
sitdown strike and an unauthorized demonstration by about one
hundred twenty black sailors. More than five hundred white men
soon circled the blacks; a group of white Marines aboard the
Constellation ran into the demonstration area armed with
nightsticks and riot batons. It took the ship's officers almost two
hours to persuade most of the whites to leave.

After this confrontation, Admiral Elmo R. Zumwalt Jr., chief of
naval operations, summoned his immediate subordinates to
Washington. He told them that they had frustrated his hopes for
lessening racial tensions by not promoting the use of the
race-relations seminars that he had developed. The navy had

over two hundred officially promulgated human relations programs, but neither the captain nor the executive officer of the *Constellation* had attended any.

About half a year before the demonstration, a human relations council had been formed aboard the *Constellation* in response to a telegram from Zumwalt. This council had met twice in six months. Its subdivision on minority affairs had never held a single meeting. At the time of the sitdown strike, only two black sailors recognized the chairman of the council or the chairman of the subdivision by name or face.

At the Washington meeting after the strike, Zumwalt argued that shipboard officers had to make better use of available race relations training and consult the navy's minority-affairs assistance officers on a continuing basis. The *Constellation*'s black sailors were placed in the hands of Captain Robert McKenzie, commander of the North Island Naval Air Station, who ordered five teams of personnel specialists and legal advisors to discuss their grievances with them.[10]

Group cohesion waxes and wanes with changes in the environment. Tightly knit groups split, split groups reunify as participants' needs change. While much of group life is impervious to managerial control, supervisors can set climates that decrease intergroup hostility. They can encourage social interaction between groups.

Informal Leaders

Whenever groups form, some administrators assume a more active role than others. They stand at the center of the group's communication network, participating in most conversations, initiating and receiving a greater number of messages than other members. Such administrators have great influence with colleagues who feel they know the score. Friends seek their advice and follow their directives.

Administrators who have high status with their peers are called *informal group leaders*. Their rank on the agency's formal hierarchy is identical to that of the people who work alongside them; they have no formal authority over their friends. Their influence stems from their personality or experience. The group confers informal leadership status on them and can withdraw it at any time. In order to maintain their dominant position, leaders must be willing and able to satisfy the members' needs for friendship, assistance, and protection.

Groups with a single leader are rare. Most have several, each with influence in a different area. Frequent choices for positions of leadership are administrators who possess one or more of the following characteristics:

1. high seniority—they help the group solve work-related problems by explaining how the unit handled similar situations in the past.

2. sympathetic personalities—they give colleagues personal advice (à la Dear Abby).

3. vim and vigor—they deliver pep talks when the unit hits a snag or a deadline looms.

4. speaking ability—they serve as the group's "ambassador" to the bureau chief and other outsiders.

Leadership is subject specific. Each informal leader has his own sphere of expertise and influence. For example, colleagues in a public health agency consult Dr. Smith about laboratory procedures because she has an extensive background in chemistry. But they listen to Dr. Jones' opinions about the new director because Jones is considered a shrewd judge of character.

Within their area of specialization, leaders play a crucial role in interpreting formal orders. Their perception of directives has a major impact on how thoroughly their friends obey hierarchical commands.

For example, let us assume Jack Lee, a programmer in an agency's Electronic Data Processing (EDP) unit, receives a memorandum which states that by a certain date an identification card must be worn at all times. Lee thinks nothing of the order. Later, he lunches with Sally Kleist, a friend and co-worker whose opinion he respects. As they discuss the memorandum, Kleist complains bitterly about the restriction on personal liberty. Presto, Jack Lee feels he has a legitimate gripe.

Reading the memorandum alone, Jack Lee had no objections. But his respect for his colleague's opinion weighed heavily in changing his mind. Opinion leaders often exert this type of influence through informal contacts and off-the-record conversations. (However, their impact may help as well as hinder agency operations.)

Informal leaders also play a crucial role in ordering the group's own communication network. Generally they adhere enthusiastically to grapevine norms. However, they make excellent agents of change if they think that co-workers ought to interact in new ways. An administrator with a long record of peer respect has a better chance of inducing his friends to change their behavior patterns than a regular group member, a deviant, or an isolate. When he offers proposals, some group members will accept them because they agree with their contents; others will concur because they value the leader's friendship or respect his intuition.

If you want to influence a work unit, find the informal leaders. Persuade them to accept your arguments. Then let the informal leaders convince the rest of the group.

PROFESSIONAL GROUPS

Most of the literature on agency groups deals with blue-collar, clerical, and service positions. Less has been written about informal communication among professionals, the members of occupations that traditionally require extended university training such as educational administrators, urban planners, engineers, doctors, lawyers, scientists, and accountants.[11]

This lack of research is unfortunate because the number of public agency professionals is increasing dramatically. Between 1960 and 1976 the number of bureaucrats classified by the census as "professional, technical and kindred" doubled from 2.6 to 5.4 million. This means that over one-third of all civilian government workers now belong to professions or related technical fields.[12]

Because professionals occupy crucial roles in policy development, it is useful to describe their unique informal communication networks. These emerge out of the professionals' special educational background and relationship with the agency in which they work.

Backgrounds

Professionals enter public agencies with a world view they have received in school. Their training stresses the authority of knowledge and the legitimacy of status based on education and the qualification to perform specialized tasks. (The doctor has a right to higher status than the nurse; the engineer has a right to higher status than the technician.)

Professionals are taught that they belong to a unique group—the worldwide fraternity of doctors, lawyers, educational administrators, physicists, foresters, etc. Praise or censure is most valid when it comes from professional peers. One professional can only be judged by another, who is the only person qualified to know what constitutes an appropriate professional act.

Professional schools stress that their graduates' principal satisfaction should come from meeting the high standards of their field. Throughout their careers, professionals are expected to maintain contact with these standards by joining professional organizations, attending their meetings, and subscribing to their journals.

Professional education stresses that conferences and journals are the principal channels for information exchange. They create a wide network of professionals who interact together.

Conference panels and journal articles apprise members of technical advances in the field. Informal meeting chit-chat gives colleagues working in geographically dispersed locations an opportunity to renew acquaintances and exchange information about their personal and professional lives.

The ethos of professional training assumes that practitioners do not have to turn to their co-workers in the agency for companionship and support. Rather, a sense of community and identity can emerge from professional associations. The group consists of the peers with whom the professional interacts at meetings. The informal leaders are the most distinguished practitioners of their calling (the leading professors, the authors of the most influential articles). When they criticize an agency's procedures, the professionals who work in the bureau re-evaluate their own behavior.

Professional education also stresses loyalty to a discipline rather than to the organization where the discipline is practiced. This creates difficulty for professionals who work on multidisciplinary agency teams where engineers may have to interact with geologists or chemists.

Split groups often develop in these situations. All unit members interact on a formal basis, but during lunch geologists sit at one table and chemists discuss their professional shop-talk at another. Each group seeks recruits who share its own professional socialization and therefore many of its norms and values.

Relation to the Agency

The most successful professionals rarely spend their entire careers working in one agency. They view each bureau that employs them as a place to exercise their talents. But they reserve their highest dedication for their careers as a whole, of which work in any particular department forms only a part.

Top professionals are cosmopolitans.[13] They move easily between positions in different agencies and even between the public and private sectors. Influential lawyers regularly shuttle between jobs on Wall Street and Washington. The same two-way traffic allows professors to move freely from universities to policy-making positions in business and government. Similarly, today's accountant for Peat, Marwick may be tomorrow's head of a state or local audit bureau.

This mobility augments the professional's need for an informal group that transcends a single unit's boundaries. It reinforces the academic ethos that puts a premium on nation-wide associations and conferences featuring participants from many institutions. A mobile administrator is more likely to change his own attitude if top professionals criticize agency policy. After all, his association with the department may end after two or three years but his relations with the professional brotherhood are lifelong.

Professional Elites

A growing number of agencies have a professional elite; bureaucrats with a specific educational background monopolize all the senior positions. They make essential decisions and determine key personnel policies, hiring criteria, and standards for advancement. In order to move up in the hierarchy, one has to be a member of that profession. For example, doctors dominate the Public Health Service, lawyers hold key positions in the Justice Department, engineers control state highway bureaus.[14]

When a bureaucracy chooses its leaders from a single professional field, its policy is made by people who share a view of the world and the agency's place in it. This can lead to a system of closed management, for all decision makers approach problems from a similar perspective shaped to a large extent by their professional education, prior professional experience, and the opinions of outstanding professional colleagues. Like communicates with like in each agency.

Professional elites tend to be defensive and conservative about agency programs. They are often suspicious and even hostile to innovations proposed by laymen or members of other professions. For instance, educational administrators say that parents do not understand how to run schools; some doctors argue that people without medical training cannot administer public health clinics. By assuming these kinds of attitudes, the professional elite identifies the work of the agency with the profession.

A closed elite may unconsciously use the agency to further professional goals rather than those set by the legislature. As political scientist Richard Stillman asks, "What insures that professionals will maintain the broad public view, rather than become narrow special interests seeking only their own self-advancement?"[15]

For example, shortly after World War II, Irving Langmuir (a chemist at General Electric) developed strategies for seeding clouds in order to blunt hurricanes. The meteorologists who dominated the U.S. Weather Bureau found Langmuir's claims incredible and labelled him a poacher on their professional terrain. Despite the fact that Langmuir held a Nobel Prize, the Weather Bureau's chief felt that he had to defend the meteorologists on his staff against this chemist outsider. He spoke out against cloud seeding—and set the field of weather modification back by at least a decade.[16]

Political leaders who want rapid change and innovation in agencies appoint to high positions officials who are not members of that department's particular elite. Thus, a mayor who wants an innovative welfare agency might appoint an M.B.A. as commissioner—rather than the traditional Master of Social Welfare (M.S.W.).

A professionally integrated set of administrators brings diverse perspectives to problem solving. The greater the number of viewpoints, the more likely the agency is to innovate, since by exchanging information, specialists from different fields stimulate each other's thinking.[17]

INTEGRATING GROUP NORMS AND AGENCY GOALS

The relationship between informal groups and an agency's mission is complex. Group norms influence how staff behave and therefore modify an agency's productivity. But their impact may be positive or negative, depending on the particular group and its relations with the hierarchy and the organization as a whole.

On the positive side, morale is higher in cohesive units. Administrators gain social satisfaction from coming to work; turnover and absenteeism are lower than where groups are weak. Greater cohesiveness also makes supervisors' jobs easier because they are not required to repeat information for every employee. The grapevine acts as a conduit.

Loyalty to the group gives employees an additional reason for performing effectively. Studies of combat effectiveness in the American and German armies in World War II show that soldiers performed well out of loyalty to their friends more than out of identification with national war objectives.[18]

On the negative side, groups often impose "bogeys" or informal limits on output. Librarians who interact frequently are likely to catalogue the same number of books; social workers who lunch and chat together often complete the same number of assignments. When managers demand an increase in productivity, they find that the group rallies around its norm. Employees who surpass the informal limit are treated as deviants and ostracized or needled.

Groups also have a vested interest in the status quo. They resist innovation when they feel change impairs their status or disrupts established social ties. Administrators may resist the installation of a sorely needed computer because they fear it means the loss of jobs. They fight a transfer system that sends friends to geographically dispersed locations.

A particular group's effect on agency goals depends largely on the manager's policy for communicating with subordinates. Despite the tremendous amount of paperwork generated by agencies, managers often give too little information to staff. They introduce changes without first ascertaining the questions subordinates have or the information that will motivate them to comply.

Staff learn about the change through a memorandum that tells them *what* to do—but not *why*. The manager simply outlines the steps *they* must follow to implement his plan. This type of communication creates an overheated grapevine. Staff seek information on the purpose of the change, its likely benefits and inconveniences. Since the formal channels provide no data, staff members look elsewhere. Informal group discussions center on the proposed innovations. Rumors fly; half-truths and innuendos abound. Group members discover flaws in the new plan that may not even exist. Needless to say, none of these discussions are shared with the manager. (If they were, reassurances could be provided.) The manager discovers the true state of affairs only when the half-hearted implementation is noted.

Thus dysfunctional group norms are a consequence of weak managerial communication strategies. When managers fail to explain the purpose and benefits of innovation, their subordinates have little reason to change their production quotas or leave their comfortable work routines.

Managers gain group cooperation by imparting sufficient information and allotting subordinates a role in making policy rather than foisting decisions on them. However not all managers are willing to increase their communication.

Many agency superiors presume that motivation among their employees comes primarily through fear. According to this view, orders are the most appropriate vertical communication, instead of requests, questions, clarifications, or assurances. Decision making cannot be shared.

This view, which psychologist Douglas McGregor calls Theory X, is based on the following premises:

1. Most people dislike work and avoid it when possible.

2. Most people must be coerced and threatened with punishment in order to make them put forth adequate effort towards achieving an agency's goals.

3. Most people avoid responsibility.[19]

Theory X clearly dictates an innate antagonism between personal desires and agency goals. If Theory X describes the world accurately, then the agenda of the informal group (with its emphasis on personal satisfaction) inherently conflicts with the formal organization's objectives. It makes no sense to hold extensive discussions with subordinates and seek their input; the group will resist change unless it is controlled.

Theory X, however, is outdated in light of current research. A more modern view, Theory Y, holds that:

1. Most people find the expenditure of effort in work as natural as play or rest.

2. Coercion is not the only means for getting adequate effort for agency goals. Employees exercise self-direction when they are committed to the organization's objectives.

3. Ego satisfaction is a significant reward for effort directed towards agency aims.

4. Most people learn, under proper conditions, to seek responsibility.[20]

Theory Y emphasizes the congruence of group and agency goals. Group members can fulfill their personal need to achieve by accepting responsibility and working together to meet agency objectives. Cohesive work groups can be a vehicle for increasing productivity and reducing resistance to change. Managers can harness the tremendous power of group norms to help the agency fulfill its mission.

The effective public manager makes organizational achievement a source of personal satisfaction. He encourages employees to develop a positive identification with the agency, a sense of personal commitment. He integrates the individual's need to achieve with the agency's formal mandate. He makes agency success an item on the group's agenda as well as on the agency's.

The manager integrates group and agency by establishing a multifaceted communication policy with: (1) extensive flow of information, and (2) participative decision making.

Information Flow

Sufficient exchange of information involves extensive vertical interaction between manager and subordinates and directed horizontal communication between administrators of equal rank.

Vertical exchange. What data should a manager communicate to employees?—ideally, all the facts and opinions they consider important and he is at liberty to reveal. If "every employee knew with certainty all that mattered to him, there would be ... no rumors of consequence."[21]

How does a manager learn what members of the unit consider important? By using two-way communication—communicating *with* subordinates rather than *to* them, discussing policy with staff in a way that brings questions to the surface where they can be answered. The two-way communicator encourages unit administrators to probe announcements and lay any fears or uncertainties on the table.

Administrators can exchange information with colleagues and the unit chief at planned staff meetings. If speaking arrangements are deliberately kept informal, then communication patterns soon approximate those of the group's private chats. Employees raise genuine fears; colleagues amplify and challenge each other's opinions. The informal group leader(s) assumes a major role.

Two-way communicators take care not to dominate the conversation. They spend at least fifty percent of their time receiving information. Before they answer an employee's question, they ask themselves: Do I fully understand that question? Will the information I impart answer the question actually being raised? To the extent possible, employees are encouraged to repeat questions for which they do not receive adequate replies.[22]

A manager's ability to elicit questions depends on rapport with staff. If a unit head is generally aloof or critical, employees will be guarded. If the boss dismisses confessions of fear by saying, "Oh, c'mon now," or "That's no problem," few further admissions will follow. Only when subordinates are certain that the manager sincerely wants objections will open meetings bring any substantial changes.

A subordinate once commented about Bob Rickles, a former New York City air resources commissioner, "I can walk in any time and say I've got a problem or I don't know how to handle a guy, and he is always available."[23] Two-way communication flows when staff can repeat that comment.

Horizontal exchange. Administrators also need frequent opportunities for communication with peers in other units, stimulating discussion among groups working on related projects. This horizontal interaction increases the amount of information employees receive about overall agency goals; it diminishes *suboptimization,* a process whereby a group becomes more concerned with its own specialty than with fulfilling the agency's mission.

Crossfertilization of intellect is especially important for professionals who often see the whole world through the eyes of one discipline. Rosalyn Yalow, 1977 Nobel Prize winner in Physiology and Medicine, notes that interdisciplinary cooperation is essential at the Veterans Administration Medical Center where she works. Yalow credits the success of her research unit to all its members exchanging ideas with practitioners in physics, mathematics, and medicine.[24]

Extensive intergroup communication can unfreeze resistance to change. When one unit rejects necessary innovation, the manager can arrange information exchanges with equivalent units in other agencies that have recently implemented similar policies. Even a group that tunes out the manager is likely to listen to the positive experiences of peers in other departments.

Participative Decision Making

Giving the group an opportunity to participate in making decisions increases loyalty to the organization. Few people work up enthusiasm for rules that are imposed on them. Almost everyone can obey directives they have fashioned themselves.

When public agency managers thrust policy on subordinates, the group increases its cohesion by adopting a united, negative stance. Informal leaders demonstrate their power by urging half-hearted obedience. However, when the manager presents a problem and asks the unit to solve it, group members demonstrate their cohesiveness by working together. Informal leaders show their mettle by generating effective solutions.

Units that develop strategies have a stake in their implementation. When an employee disobeys a rule set by the manager, his friends offer protection. An employee who refuses to accept group-initiated policy has no such refuge; he gets pressure from both colleagues and the unit chief.

Group input is not appropriate for all decisions. (A manager does not ask a group to decide which of its members should be let go.) But industrial research indicates that groups often do a good job of working out their own division of labor, schedules, and control patterns; they set goals that are surprisingly high.[25] Employees who participate in decision making are far better at making choices when emergencies arise. They take greater responsibility for solving problems.

Stimulating participation. Managers do not stimulate participation by abdicating authority and saying "Take charge." That path only leads to confusion and eventual bitterness. (It also makes one wonder how the manager earns a salary.)

Participative decision making requires extensive interaction between the manager and the unit. It is the manager's responsibility to state the problem, identify the group's choice in terms of "allowable" solutions, and clarify limits based on:

1. permissibility (e.g., What range of solutions will top officials accept? What range is politically feasible? What range is in the public interest?);

2. fiscal resources (How much money is available?);

3. time (How long a period does the group have to find a solution?);

4. previous agency commitments; and

5. available information.[26]

If there are plausible solutions that the agency cannot accept, the manager identifies them along with the reasons for their unacceptability. At no time is the group allowed to believe that it has more (or less) power than it actually has.

Sharing information. Participative decision making also requires sharing information. Managers contribute their insights; the employees, theirs. At staff meetings, managers maximize diversity of inputs by:

1. paying special attention to newcomers and isolates;
2. waiting out pauses and lapses in interaction;
3. restating ideas contributed by others (sometimes in a clearer form); and
4. summarizing discussion as the need arises.

One of the advantages of encouraging group participation is the diversity of insights an entire unit brings to bear on a problem. The manager has a greater amount of information on the relationship of different solutions to overall agency goals. Each administrator has greater know-how about a unique aspect of day-to-day implementation. A multiplicity of participants ensures a multiplicity of perspectives. Better decisions tend to emerge because more varied data are used in building them. As U.S. Congressman Robert Michel (R-Ill.) says, "I don't know how you can ever just out of thin air dream up a . . . proposal without going to those of your people who work directly on a day-to-day basis with the thing."[27] The entire staff has valuable information to communicate.

Accepting decisions. The manager must accept the group's consensus if it is within the limits set. It is unlikely that the group's decision will be a photocopy of the manager's own pet plan. The solution may not even be one that he particularly favors.

Nevertheless, the time to limit employee discretion is at the start. A public agency manager has a right—even an obligation—to keep the group out of areas that are not its proper concern. But once the group begins its deliberations, the manager waives any veto power as long as the employees accept the ground rules.

Managers who try to manipulate a group covertly or withdraw

authority that has been delegated deserve all the hostility they will undoubtedly receive. A manager who thinks that employees can be manipulated without their realizing it simply assumes that they are dumber than he is—a dangerous assumption for any agency administrator to make.

The effective manager understands that an adequate solution which has the group's support will be more enthusiastically implemented than a "pet" proposal unilaterally imposed. A choice the manager perceives as only "acceptable" may thus be best for the agency in the long run.

The need to accept solicited decisions underscores the importance of setting careful ground rules. If managers only seek the group's suggestions, they must clearly explain that they retain final authority. Once they ask the unit to find the solution, they must abide by its choice.

A word of caution. Some commentators suggest that interactive decision making is a magic glue that always binds group to agency. In actuality, participation is a technique that is appropriate in many situations but inappropriate in others. Its success is directly tied to the nature of the group and the manager's personal attributes and interactions with subordinates. Effective participative decision making requires a manager with a repertoire of leadership qualities and the ability to use each as it fits the situation.

In order to continue our discussion on participation, we have to examine what it means to *lead* in public agencies. Leadership and manager-subordinate communication are interdependent concepts. Appropriate leadership is a prerequisite for effective vertical communication, and effective communication is a necessary condition for appropriate leadership.

3

Communication and Leadership

A political commentator once noted that leadership is a quality nobody notices until it is gone. When an organization runs smoothly, few people praise its leaders; but let performance slip and calls are heard for dynamic leading.

Our society perceives a lack of leadership in public agencies. We have no dearth of bodies available to fill high administrative commands. What we seem to lack are genuine leaders who arouse devotion and enthusiasm. We need top public officials with the zeal, ardor, earnestness, and intensity to inspire employees.

What Is Leadership?

The term *leading* appears in the English language as early as 1300. Although it has been used steadily since, modern social scientists are in fairly good accord about its meaning. Stogdill defines it as "the process (act) of influencing the activities of an organized group in its effort towards goal setting and goal achievement."[1]

Starling views leading as the act of "influencing the activities of a group in efforts towards goal attainment in a given situation,"[2] while Koontz and O'Donnell define it as acting to help "a group attain objectives with the maximum application of its capabilities."[3] All these definitions indicate that leading involves persuasion or influence. It is a resource for management that begins when *authority* leaves off.

Leadership and Authority

A public manager's authority (or right to control) stems from a job title. Legislative statutes and agency regulations define the duties and responsibilities of each position and which offices have legal sanction to give orders to others. The authority of a public manager's commands depends on his place in the hierarchy, not on personal attributes. When two managers have identical job titles, their authority is always equivalent since it adheres to the position itself and not the officeholder.

Leadership differs from authority. It is based on the manager's personal ability to motivate the group by controlling valued resources. Two managers with identical job titles can have widely varying leadership potentials; they may differ in their ability to make the goals of the staff coincide with the organization's aims.

Authority alone is rarely sufficient to get a unit to put forth maximum effort. Managers with a clear, legal right to command are sometimes incredulous at the disobedience or half-hearted acquiescence that subordinates manifest. An assistant to the director of New York City's Bureau of Methadone Maintenance summed up the pattern in his office:

> No one will follow procedures! You can lay them out step-by-step and people don't do it. We have . . . a very clearcut paper flow, a very specific description . . . but nobody takes the time to do it properly.[4]

The inadequacy of authority as a resource for control underscores the importance of leadership. Koontz and O'Donnell suggest that without effective leadership, employees only use sixty percent of their capabilities.[5] Dynamic leadership is required to produce the remaining forty percent.

Leadership Roles

Effective leaders perform two functions. They structure the unit's formal activities, thereby establishing strategies for meeting agency objectives. They also engage in personal relations with the group, encouraging warmth and rapport and extensive two-way communication.

One reason for the present scarcity of public leaders may be the dual nature of the task. Effective leaders need technical skills in order to assign and structure work. They also need interpersonal competence—the ability to deal with people. Effectiveness in the first area is insufficient to motivate a group to perform at maximum capability.

LEADERSHIP THEORY AND RESEARCH

A considerable volume of leadership research has been written since the beginning of World War II. Analyzing some of it affords an opportunity to consider in greater detail the behavior patterns that produce effective leadership and the ways managers can cultivate these patterns.

The Trait Approach

Prior to 1950, leadership research was based largely on an attempt to identify the traits or personality characteristics that leaders possess. Scholars analyzed whether effective leadership depended on religious inspiration, high I.Q., great physical strength, or other personal qualities.

In general, this line of study was not fruitful. Researchers failed to produce a set of personality traits that invariably discriminates between leaders and nonleaders.[6] (It is difficult to see precisely which characteristics George Washington, Joseph Stalin, Napoleon Bonaparte, Mahatma Gandhi, Martin Luther King, Abraham Lincoln, and Adolf Hitler share.) Also the studies gave no guide as to how much of any desirable trait a manager should have.

Styles of Leadership

By 1950 most social scientists had abandoned the search for leadership traits. They shifted instead to describing particular styles of leadership in the hope of finding which was most effective.

This approach had been pioneered in 1939 by psychologist Kurt Lewin who identified three distinct ways of leading, each with its own "typical" behavior patterns and communication strategies.[7] Lewin labelled these three styles: authoritarian, democratic, and laissez faire.

Authoritarian. Authoritarian or directive leaders dominate decision making and activity determination for the unit. They emphasize one-way communication, dictating tasks and techniques unilaterally. Their pronouncements tend to be task rather than rapport oriented; in general, they remain aloof from camaraderie or personal participation with staff.

Democratic. Democratic leaders place greater emphasis on group participation. They stress two-way communication with their role being to describe organizational goals, offer technical advice, and identify a framework for staff decisions. Democratic leaders are task and rapport oriented. They consider the personal needs of staff as well as completion of legislatively mandated functions.

Laissez faire. Laissez faire or free rein leaders allow staff almost complete freedom in decision making; their participation is minimal. Laissez faire leaders give few directives and rarely supply information unless asked. They make no attempt to participate in the group's social concerns.

Laissez faire leaders are relatively uncommon in public agencies. Accordingly, most of the public management literature ignores this style and concentrates on debating the merits of directive and participative approaches.

DEMOCRATIC STYLE AND EFFECTIVENESS

During the 1950s and 1960s, management specialists investigated the advantages of democratic leading, spurring a trend away from close direction and towards greater participation.

Likert's "Participative Group" System

For three decades, Rensis Likert and his associates at the University of Michigan studied leadership in public and private organizations.[8] They found that managers using a "participative group" approach had the greatest success. Their departments tended to be most effective at setting and achieving objectives. Likert attributes their success to three factors: delegation, general supervision, and extensive exchange of information.

Delegation. The participative leader delegates responsibility to unit members, thus increasing their sense of autonomy. While the leader sets goals and fixes limits, the group is still encouraged to select its own strategies for meeting objectives.

General supervision. Effective leaders supervise by overseeing results, i.e., they check whether employees meet predetermined goals. Participative leaders do not waste time running from "crisis" to "crisis" giving specific instructions and then checking to see that employees obey each to the letter. Time saved is spent planning and improving rapport.

Information exchange. Participative leaders provide staff with an informational framework that enables them to cope on their own. They mobilize their units by giving each member enough data to feel a sense of control.

This strategy has two benefits. It leaves managers free to handle the long-range facets of their jobs without interruptions from staff members who need routine information. It also develops the staff's ability to make decisions and increases their pride in the unit's accomplishments.

The Managerial Grid

Robert Blake and Jane Srygley Mouton's managerial grid is a device for dramatizing the need for democratic leadership.[9] Blake and Mouton argue that leadership style rests primarily on a *concern for production* and a *concern for people*. A leader may be highly interested in increasing production (meeting the goal) or relatively uninterested; concern for subordinates may also be high or low.

The managerial grid is a pictorial strategy for identifying the interaction of high, intermediate, and low degrees of each orientation (see figure 3.1). The 1,1 "impoverished" manager lacks much interest in productivity or people. The 9,1 "task-centered" manager is twin to Lewin's authoritarian leader, highly oriented towards meeting goals but relatively unconcerned with his impact on subordinates. The 1,9 "country club" manager is preoccupied solely with human relations to the detriment of productivity. The 9,9 "team" manager is the true democratic leader who enhances productivity by giving subordinates a psychological stake in agency performance.

Blake and Mouton argue that team management maximizes goal attainment by increasing the employee's effort, creativity, and commitment. They have so much faith in participative leadership that they label it "the key to strengthening . . . political democracy."[10]

SITUATIONAL LEADERSHIP

The literature on leadership styles suggests that there is an easy answer to the complex question: How should I lead? It pigeonholes influence patterns into three separate boxes and labels the "democratic" bin as the most appropriate.

Prior to 1950, most managers in public and private organizations made decisions unilaterally. The literature on participative management led to a welcome decrease in authoritarianism and one-way communication. Soon, however, the increase in staff participation brought a new problem into focus: reconciling democratic leadership and managerial control. High officials were often uncertain how to behave. Many were torn between being "strong" and being "permissive," with the new literature pushing them in one direction and old habits and experience urging them toward the other. There were times when they found group participation appropriate and other times when it seemed to be a device for avoiding responsibility.

Many officials felt instinctively that leadership was too complex an activity to have one universally correct style. They wanted a framework that took into account the wide variety of environments a public manager encounters, recognizing that there are times when direction is appropriate and other times

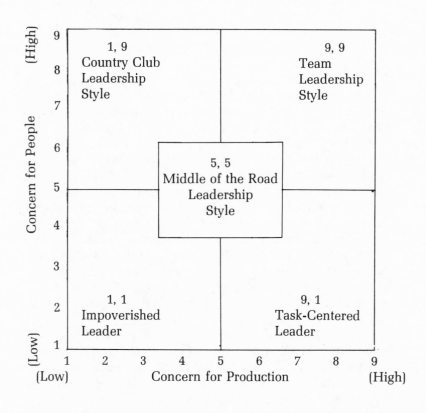

FIG. 3.1. THE MANAGERIAL GRID

Source: Adapted from Robert R. Blake and Jane S. Mouton, *The Managerial Grid* (Houston, Tex: Gulf Publishing Co., 1964), p. 10.

43

when it makes sense to encourage group participation. A theory was needed that delineated the effect that the particular situation or contingency had on choosing an effective leadership pattern.

Leadership as a Continuum

The first widely accepted contingency framework was offered by Tannenbaum and Schmidt.[11] In a pathbreaking critique they rejected the traditional concept of three separate leadership styles, preferring instead to characterize leadership as a continuum.

An infinite variety of points or behavior patterns separates absolute boss-centered and subordinate-centered leadership. Every manager chooses from an enormous range of alternatives in relating to employees. The ensuing patterns cannot be lumped into three discrete categories because each manager's behavior is slightly different from any colleague's. Two leaders we label "democratic" almost certainly behave differently in their day-to-day routines. (One gives subordinates slightly greater leeway; the other explains goals in somewhat greater detail.) Given this bewildering variety of patterns, it is absurd to insist that one style works best in every situation.

Tannenbaum and Schmidt argue that no all-purpose leadership style exists. The appropriate pattern varies, depending on forces in the manager, the subordinates, and the situation. The sensitive official assesses all of these factors before deciding how to lead in a given contingency.

Forces in the manager. A manager's behavior is influenced by four forces acting in his own personality, including

1. value systems,
2. trust in subordinates,
3. leadership inclinations, and
4. tolerance for ambiguity.

Managers with low trust and intolerance for ambiguity are more comfortable in highly directive roles. Urging them to encourage greater participation can be counter-productive; such managers often become "plated" leaders—democratic silver on top, authoritarian brass through and through.

Their behavior creates confusion because their style shifts arbitrarily. Their staff meetings engender bitterness and cynicism because the managers promise subordinates greater freedom and responsibility than they are ready to deliver. Tannenbaum and Schmidt argue that the agency is often best off if it allows these officials to follow their natural bent and places them in units where the employees and the situation call for directive leadership.

Forces in the subordinate. Employees also are influenced by many personality variables. Not all groups want to participate in decision making; substantial differences exist in the kind of responsibility people want to accept on the job.

A specialist in personnel management was once assigned an elderly secretary in a federal agency. Being a firm believer in participative management, he explained the background of every letter he dictated and urged the secretary to draft some of the letters herself. At last, she replied, "I'm not paid to do that kind of work! That's your job."[12]

Some agency employees are accustomed to the authoritarian approach. They expect the supervisor to make all the decisions. They are disappointed if input is solicited or goal-directed two-way communication is encouraged.

Generally, employees want participative management when they have

1. a readiness to assume responsibility;
2. a tolerance for ambiguity;
3. a high need for independence;
4. an interest in the problem and the agency's goals; and
5. the necessary knowledge and experience to contribute fruitfully.

Tannenbaum and Schmidt argue that participative patterns are only appropriate when these conditions are met; at other times, managers may have no short-range immediate alternatives to directive leading. In the long run, managers may be able to enhance the employee's psychological skills (e.g., readiness to assume responsibility) through careful training (see chapter 10).

Forces in the situation. Certain forces in the work environment affect the proper leadership pattern. Situations with intense time pressures cry out for boss-centered decisions. A lieutenant cannot call a staff meeting before ordering the combat infantry to advance. Fire chiefs direct their crews at the scene of a fire; they cannot consult or solicit opinions.

Another important situational force is a manager's relations with his or her own superiors. Every agency executive (no matter what his rank) has a boss of his own and must be aware of his expectations. If directive leadership prevails throughout an agency, the lone participative manager may find that he encounters problems in dealing with his superiors and that this diminishes his effectiveness. Even if he wants to encourage participation, he may be more productive making some decisions unilaterally.

Tannenbaum and Schmidt stress that the successful leader is aware of all the forces influencing his behavior. He chooses leadership patterns based on knowledge of his own personality, the needs of his subordinates, and the particular environment in which he operates.

Leadership and the Life Cycle

A second theory of situational leadership is Hersey and Blanchard's "life cycle" paradigm.[13] Building on Tannenbaum and Schmidt's model, they argue that success at leading is comparable to success at being a parent: in both, the proper approach depends on the "maturity" of the people being led.

Suppose a friend asks you, "How can I be a good parent? How much independence can I give my child? How much direction shall I offer?" You cannot answer these questions unless you know how old the child is and how much responsibility he is capable of assuming. A parental style that works well at one stage of a child's life may fail miserably at another. Thus, an infant requires parent-centered leadership in that the mother or father must make critical decisions about food, sleep, and medicine unilaterally. As the child matures to where he can handle increased responsibility, successful parents change their style and invite participation in decision making.

By the time the child reaches early adulthood, he can make

most decisions for himself. Wise parents shift their style once again and assume a laissez faire attitude. They remain available to give information and encouragement but they refrain from imposing solutions.

According to Hersey and Blanchard, the situation is similar for agency managers. We cannot tell a manager how to lead unless we know something about the maturity (or willingness to shoulder responsibility) of the administrators in the unit. A group with little ability or desire to accept responsibility requires directive leadership. As its maturity grows (through training and extensive two-way communication), the manager can give the members more opportunities to propose procedural solutions.

A few groups are mature enough to make most decisions for themselves. Professionals with great commitment to their work are only comfortable with leaders who provide minimal supervision.

For example, doctors in public hospitals prefer laissez faire administrators; they want executives who communicate information when asked but refrain from interfering in patient-care decisions. Scientists at the National Bureau of Standards and other research-oriented agencies take pride in selecting their own projects and the methodologies for carrying them out.

To sum up: Hersey and Blanchard emphasize how crucial the needs of followers are in selecting a leadership pattern. Effective leading depends on the manager's understanding the unit's need to assume responsibility and a willingness to shift leadership style (to the degree permitted by his own personality) in order to meet the group's expectations and desires.

Life Cycle Theory and the Hierarchy of Needs

The life cycle theory ties leadership to motivation, recognizing that different people seek satisfaction of different needs. The pioneering work of psychologist Abraham Maslow sheds additional light on this point. According to Maslow, a hierarchy of needs exists in that desires that motivate any person at a given point in time depend upon the needs that are already satisfied.[14] An analysis of the relationship between Maslow's work and life cycle theory explains why various groups are at different stages of maturity and why democratic leadership is the most appropriate in most, but not all, modern agency units.

Maslow's hierarchy. Maslow's hierarchy of needs begins with the desire for physical sustenance, safety, and security, and is followed by the sense of belonging, esteem, and finally self-actualization (or reaching one's full potential).

Since every person's most fundamental desire is for physical sustenance (e.g., food, water, shelter), this must be satisfied before any other motivations will appear. After physical needs are met, an individual then becomes concerned with achieving safety and security. (Thus administrators who feel that their current salaries provide adequate food and shelter will probably turn their attention to securing pension benefits to protect retirement.) Once the administrator feels secure, the need for friendship emerges. The employee who feels reasonably safe in a position concentrates on winning the acceptance of co-workers.

The fourth step in Maslow's sequence is the desire to gain the respect of others, or in terms of an administrator to have colleagues say that you analyze budgets brilliantly or really know how to write a fundable proposal. The fifth stage is to gain self-respect—to show yourself that you can do a fine job and gain pleasure from it.

The type of leadership given administrators need depends on their primary motivations. Hersey and Blanchard argue that directive leadership is necessary when employees are primarily concerned with physical needs and security (a situation that is not prevalent in today's government agency). These employees are not very committed to the work itself and therefore are not likely to want a large share of responsibility.

Democratic leadership is appropriate for employees who want primarily to satisfy social needs. Participation gives them a chance to interact with colleagues in goal-directed situations.

Administrators primarily concerned with satisfying the need for esteem or self-actualization are most comfortable with free rein leaders. Their desire to assume responsibility is great because they derive satisfaction from the work itself. Their motivation is intrinsic.

Life Cycle Theory in Public Agencies

The needs that motivate public administrators today differ from those that prodded their predecessors fifty or sixty years ago. Few people who work in public agencies are worried about meeting their most basic needs. Governmental salaries may never assure instant wealth but they do provide adequate physical sustenance. Civil service commissions and public employee unions guarantee unprecedented job security. Thus, most administrators come to their jobs ready to satisfy their need to belong.

The growing number of professionals in public service suggests that some administrators are also motivated by the need for esteem and self-actualization. Cosmopolitan professionals in particular seek fulfillment in their jobs; they want a "calling or vocation in the old sense . . . which they work at and which they love, so that the work–joy dichotomy disappears."[15]

As the forces motivating administrators change, managers must accommodate their leadership patterns. Because public administrators who expect authoritarian leadership are becoming increasingly rare, directive leadership is appropriate in fewer and fewer bureaus.

Furthermore, opportunities for effective group participation are growing. Democratic communication patterns are the most important for the modern agency manager to master. (When we say that the manager needs a repertoire of patterns we mean primarily a repertoire within the democratic range.) In research and other highly professionalized units, free rein leading is another appropriate style.

The present emphasis on situational leadership stresses that leading is an art; performance is contingent on matching style and situation. Some public managers who succeed in one environment may fail in another because their leadership qualities only match those needed in the first instance. As Fiedler notes: "it is simply not meaningful to speak of an effective . . . or an ineffective leader; we can only speak of a leader who tends to be effective in one situation."[16]

Accordingly, we cannot speak of a single leadership

communication pattern that is effective for all public agency managers. The "correct" communication technique depends on a host of contingencies. The most appropriate generalization is: a communication strategy works if it keeps manager and unit "tuned" to the same message. Frequently (but not always) the style that does this best is extensive two-way interaction and group decision making.

The modern public executive has to develop a repertoire of oral and written communication strategies, each designed to get messages across in a particular situation. Managers must always ask themselves: "How does my message look to the audience? Do my words take into account their motivations? Am I coming across with maximum clarity?"

Clarity is a prerequisite for effective leadership communication. Yet how often public administrators fail to communicate in a way that subordinates can understand. It is hard to exaggerate the amount of misunderstanding caused by partial or blocked exchanges of information. All too often, agency managers recall failures in terms of "If I had only said it this way rather than that!"

Communication blockages constitute one of the most serious problems in agency leading.[17] Blockages prevent decision makers from getting sufficient information to select the appropriate alternative; they hinder subordinate administrators from receiving the data they need to carry out agency policy.

Before public executives develop various strategies for oral and written communication, they ought to have some understanding of the kinds of blockages that occur in agency exchanges. They ought to know tactics for hurdling these barriers.

Unit II analyzes five common communication barriers: language, frame of reference, status differences, geographical distance, and the pressure of other work. A separate chapter describes why each barrier hinders communication and how the manager can avoid some of its dysfunctional effects. Then units III and IV concentrate on developing leadership communication skills for specific oral and written situations.

Summing Up
Concepts for Review;
Problems and Exercises

51

Leadership
  authoritarian or directive
  democratic or participative
  laissez faire or free rein
Managerial grid
Contingency theories
  leadership as a continuum
  leadership and the life cycle
Hierarchy of needs

PROBLEMS AND EXERCISES

1. Margaret Jones and Larry Pulaski are administrators in the Small Business Administration. Margaret asks Larry to develop a report on loans to small businesses. (The person who generally handles this is on vacation.) Larry says that he will write the report next week. Are Margaret's request and Larry's agreement examples of formal or informal communication? Why?

2. Over pizza and Coke, Joe Torelli tells Carol Blair that the new unit chief is a stickler for details. Assuming Joe's information is *false*, can this lunchtime gossip affect Carol's on-the-job productivity? Why?

3. A county social service department delegates authority to process client applications from the casework supervisors to the individual social workers. What changes are likely to occur in the department's flexibility and uniformity of response?

4. No minutes or notes are taken at a staff meeting held by a fire captain and ten lieutenants. The captain simply outlines new procedures and asks the lieutenants to pass them on to their crews.

   a. Will all the crews receive the same procedures?

   b. How can the fire captain increase uniformity?

5. A police department in a large northeastern city wants to use one-person patrol cars in certain districts. (Currently, all cars carry two officers regardless of the area or time of day and the department considers this an expensive allocation of resources.)

The rank and file are against the change. Their union contends that vehicles must carry two officers in order to ensure their safety; an officer riding alone might be ambushed or subject to attack.

The police commissioner writes a memorandum to all members of the department, telling them that one-officer cars do not imperil safety. Nineteen other large cities use one-person vehicles without suffering high on-the-job injuries. The police commissioner is certain that his memorandum will make a dent in the rank and file's attitude. Two weeks after he sends it, he is genuinely surprised to learn that the opposition is as vehement as ever.

    a. Why are the officers opposing the new policy? Is safety the only concern? What other benefits do they get from two-person vehicles?

    b. Assume you are the police commissioner. How would you convince the officers to accept one-person cars?

6. Jack Lynch works in the audit bureau of a federal agency. Yesterday was his first day in the field, analyzing documents in a local agency that receives federal funds.

In the morning, Jack's supervisor Jill Dalton told him to check papers from a predetermined sample. Jill then walked away without giving Jack a chance to ask any questions. Jack, however, had prior audit experience. Even though he did not talk to Jill again that morning, he was able to analyze more documents than the other auditors, all of whom checked approximately the same amount.

At twelve, all of Jack's colleagues went to lunch together. "You're coming with us, aren't you?" Bill Donahue asked. "Going to lunch together is a habit with this group." "Stick close to Bill," another auditor said. "He knows more about this job than anybody."

Jack returned to work still deep in the midst of a conversation with Bill Donahue. That afternoon, Jack analyzed fewer documents than in the morning. Jill Dalton was surprised to find that Jack was now working at the same pace as the others.

    a. What relationship exists among the auditors?

    b. What role does Bill Donahue serve for them?

    c. What factors explain the relationships that exist in the audit group?

d. What can Jill Dalton do to increase unit productivity?

7. Select a public agency in your area that allows you to observe a unit over a few weeks. (If you work in an agency, it is a logical choice.)

    a. Identify the agency's overall mission and the principal strategies it uses to achieve this goal.

    b. Identify the agency's major patterns of formal communication established by the legislature and agency regulations. How do these communication patterns help the agency reach its goal?

    c. Select one unit within the agency. Identify its primary objectives and tactics for achieving them.

    d. Identify *three* informal mechanisms that administrators in the unit use for exchanging information. Analyze how each pattern helps or hinders the unit in reaching its objectives.

    e. What type of leader is the unit manager? Is this style effective? What type of leadership would be best for this particular unit? Why? (Take into account the manager's personality, the administrators, and the situation.)

8. Re-examine the list of qualities on page 44. Then evaluate the forces in your own personality that aid or detract from your ability to function as a democratic leader.

    a. Assess your:

        1) value system (How comfortable are you sharing authority?)

        2) trust in subordinates (Do you tend to trust people with less education or experience than you have?)

        3) leadership inclination (Are you most comfortable when you direct the situation? Why?)

        4) tolerance for ambiguity (Are you comfortable in situations where you do not know the answer or the answer is in doubt?)

    b. Which forces in your personality would you like to strengthen in the next year? What are the appropriate strategies?

UNIT TWO

Hurdling Communication Barriers

4
Language

In Unit I we explained that genuine communication occurs only when a message is understood.

How public administrators shape and send their messages determines the information that the audience receives. Filtering and distortion are possible at every stage; administrators have to be on guard against the communication blockages that are only too prone to occur in agencies.

The first step in preventing misunderstanding is for the administrator to recognize that faulty use of language remains one of the most pervasive barriers to effective information exchange. Public managers invite misunderstanding when they use:

1. words that have different meanings for them and for their audience(s);

2. excessive (or inappropriate) *argot* and *jargon*; and other *gobbledygook*.

In the remainder of the chapter, we analyze why these practices cause misunderstanding and how administrators can avoid them.

WORDS AND THEIR MEANINGS

Language is a system of symbols used to express facts and emotions. However, the same symbols or words often have different meanings for different people.

For example, the unit chief tells his assistant, "Prepare a report as soon as you can." But he *means*, "Drop all other activities. Prepare it immediately!" The assistant, in the middle of analyzing a budget, thinks the manager means, "Prepare the report as soon as you finish working on the figures." When the unit chief demands the report two hours later, he is angry with the assistant for not having started it yet, and the assistant is genuinely perplexed: "If he wanted it right away, why didn't he say so?"

Legend has it that former F.B.I. Director J. Edgar Hoover's misuse of words once sent agents out on a wild goose chase. Hoover had insisted that internal memoranda have wide margins so that he could scribble comments in the empty spaces. Once he received a memorandum whose margins were particularly narrow; he sent it back immediately with the comment "Watch the borders." For the next week, F.B.I. agents fanned out on the Mexican and Canadian borders. They believed their director wanted them to keep a vigorous alert.[1]

Denotation and Connotation

The problem of choosing the correct phrase is complicated because many words carry multiple shades of meaning.[2] They have *denotations*, which are direct, explicit definitions, and *connotations*, which are overtones or associations that suggest other meanings in addition to the explicit one. For example, *cop* and *police officer* have the same explicit meaning but the latter connotes greater respect. This is also true for *politician* and *statesman*; their denotations are similar, but the second term connotes a person with intelligence and vision. The words *firm, obstinate*, and *pigheaded* are not very different in explicit meaning. Yet firmness can be a virtue; call a colleague obstinate or pigheaded and you may have a quarrel on your hands.

Some words acquire such profound connotations that we forget their explicit meanings. The terms *cur* and *bitch* are thrown around in anger quite often without anybody imagining that the recipient is a dog.

A problem arises when a word has one connotation for the communicator and another for the audience. A manager praises a subordinate by saying, "You're competent." To the manager this means, "You are really doing an outstanding job." But the subordinate may go home dejected. To him, the word *competent* means *satisfactory*. He thinks the manager has given his work a C rating.

Too many public managers only consider the connotations their words have for them. They fail to evaluate other possible interpretations and forget the old maxim: If an audience can possibly misinterpret a word, it probably will.

Stereotypes are an extreme form of connotation that distort the explicit meaning attached to a given word. When communicators stereotype, they attribute certain characteristics to a class of people or experiences. Then, they proceed to judge those people or experiences on the basis of their own attributions.

Let us assume Reginald Pringle thinks all women are indecisive. Every time he sees a woman he attributes the quality of indecisiveness to her. His unit chief, Jane Cohen, solicits input to increase morale; the next day, at the water cooler, Reginald tells his buddy, "Well, there's another woman who can't make up her own mind."

The use of stereotypes grows out of people's need for predictability. An underlying purpose of human thinking is the desire to reduce ambiguity. Stereotyping allows communicators to classify people quickly and easily; they pigeonhole millions on the basis of a few, key characteristics.

Some stereotypes are simply ludicrous—they have no objective basis in fact. Others are true for a group as a whole but are totally invalid when applied to a particular group member. Communicators make an error in logic when they *infer* that what is correct for a group is necessarily true for each individual in that whole. As a group, workers sixty years old lack the physical stamina of workers who are twenty. However, this statement in no way certifies that Ann Jones, age sixty, lacks the physical stamina to be a police officer or a forest ranger.

Stereotypes thrive on ignorance. Mingling with many types of people diminishes their use.

ARGOT AND JARGON

In a society as specialized as ours, there are thousands of different languages attached to various social networks and occupations. Professions, in particular, make use of complex, technical vocabularies called *jargon*. Lawyers have their own terminology, personnel specialists have theirs, econometricians have a vocabulary only understood by people with their education.

Within agencies, informal groups develop their own idiomatic slang called *argot*. Ability to understand this potpourri of colorful phrases is restricted to people who work in a particular unit.

Argot and jargon have legitimate, if limited, places in intragroup communication where initiator and audience understand the specialized vocabulary. Using "in" argot satisfies an employee's need to belong, reinforces a sense of self-esteem, and can contribute to increased morale. Some use of technical jargon is necessary to ensure precision in professional reports. Research papers must employ specialized vocabularies.

Neither argot nor jargon has a legitimate role in communication between groups. A problem arises when administrators become so accustomed to communicating with peers in argot or jargon that they continue the practice outside their social or professional group. The new audience is unable to understand the specialized vocabulary. It regards the message with dismay—as if it were written in Tagalog or Urdu.

The in-house argot developed by medical fraud investigators in one state social service agency was elaborate and colorful. They used the term *ping-ponging* to describe clients who visited many doctors for one complaint. *Hard duplicate* was the phrase used to identify a physician who charged the government twice for providing one service. Use of these homemade terms caused no problem as long as investigators confined it to in-house conversation. Trouble arose when the argot crept into reports sent to the district attorney's office. What was an assistant D.A. to make of the words "the client ping-ponged"? To an outsider, it seemed as irrelevant as adding "The doctor played tennis." Luckily, the agency realized quite quickly that it had a communication problem. It instituted training workshops which stressed the importance of writing in English.

GOBBLEDYGOOK

Unfortunately, big words and obscure phrases are a common feature of agency communications. A Labor Department press release refers to "transport equipment operatives," i.e., truck drivers! A public health service memorandum identifies a process of "disinsection," i.e., removing disease-carrying insects from airplanes. Message after message speaks of "utilizing resources" or "utilization of personnel." What is wrong with "using resources" or the "use of personnel"?

Some communicators use a series of esoteric phrases to belabor trivialities. The *Alaska Administrative Code* informs us that:

> (1) reshippers are shippers who transship shucked stock in original containers or shell-stock from certified shellfish shippers to other dealers or to final consumers; reshippers may not shuck or repack shellfish; (2) repackers are shippers other than the original shucker who pack shucked shellfish into containers for delivery to the consumer; shippers classified as repackers may shuck shellfish if they have the necessary facilities; a repacker may also act as a shell-stock shipper if he has the necessary facilities.[3]

Everything clear?

Semanticists use the term *gobbledygook* to denote this kind of language that contains excessive jargon or argot and verbal runaround. Gobbledygook is characterized by: (1) unnecessary sentences; (2) many polysyllabic (or big) words; (3) technical, little-known phrases; (4) overuse of abstractions; (5) confusing, overcomplex syntax; and (6) overuse of the passive voice (saying "The book was taken by him" rather than "He took the book").

Gobbledygook, by definition, contains words and syntax that tax understanding. Its use needlessly complicates the process of initiating and receiving messages. It has no legitimate place in public agencies; administrators should avoid it in all situations.

COMMUNICATING WITH AN AUDIENCE

The reasons that managers misuse language are as much psychological as technical. Too often administrators compose messages without considering whether their audience(s) will understand them.

In order for public managers to use language effectively, they must consider the audience's needs. Appropriate language varies depending on the recipient's background. Agency managers have to keep in mind the education and experience that colleagues and staff bring to the job. They must encourage sufficient two-way communication so that they know something about their subordinate's world and possible connotations they give various words and phrases. Then they can tailor messages to fit a given audience's own values, vocabulary, and mood.

In general, effective agency communicators use the most simple language that conveys their message. Any time they switch to technical terminology, they question whether the use of an occupationally restricted vocabulary is necessary for precision.

Seven rules-of-thumb are:

1. Use short sentences. Unnecessary words obscure meaning.

2. Eliminate deadwood—words that add nothing to the message. Which of the following sentences is easier to follow?

> a. The employee is commanding in her attitude but she is a rather selfish person.
>
> b. The employee is commanding, but rather selfish.

Most people prefer the second. It has a tighter structure; unnecessary words are eliminated.

3. Use short, familiar words. Say "end" rather than "terminate." Write "exit" instead of "egress."

4. Limit the use of adverbs, adjectives, and verbs ending in *ize*. Which of the following phrases is easier to read?

> a. Maximize and optimalize dynamic production capability.
>
> b. Increase production.

Remember that the next time you write a memorandum!

5. Define terms when exact meaning is essential and the

audience might interpret a word in more than one way.

6. Be as concrete and specific as possible. Vague phrases invite misunderstanding. Say "I want the report tomorrow morning" instead of "I want the report soon."

7. Repeat information that might be misinterpreted, using slightly different terms each time. If the audience misunderstands one phrase, it will get the meaning from the others.[4]

MEASURING READABILITY

Public managers should be able to evaluate the readability of their messages.[5] Experienced officials do this automatically. As they compose, they consider how the audience will interpret different words. However, new administrators often find judging readability to be quite a challenge. They are not prepared to assess the impact a message has on others.

Luckily, a simple exercise can give people feedback about their use of language. Write a paragraph on a public agency topic, gearing it to a specific audience. Then erase every fifth word. Distribute the message to members of the audience and ask them to decipher it.

The greater the proportion of people who know the missing terms, the greater your readability (for that particular audience). If few people make sense out of the message, you probably have to change your vocabulary and syntax.

Complex, statistical formulas also exist for measuring readability. An advantage of these formulas is that they correlate readability with average grade level completed, an audience characteristic that is relatively easy to calculate for agency administrators. Disadvantages are that they test syntax and length of words but not meaning or familiarity. (A familiar, multisyllabic word such as *transportation* may be easier for many people to read than esoteric, one-syllable words such as *adz* or *xaz*.[6]) Also, their use requires an expenditure of time. Mathematically calculating the readability of a training manual that will be used by several thousand clerks makes sense; calculating the readability of a memorandum does not.

The Flesch Readability Scale is probably the most popular mathematical aid.[7] To use it:

1. Select a one-hundred-word passage for every ten pages in the report.

2. Count the number of sentences or independent clauses (SEN).

3. Count the number of syllables (SYL).

4. Compute the readability score for each passage.

Flesch Score $= 206.835 - SYL \times 0.846 - (100/SEN) \times 1.015$

5. Compute the average readability score if there is more than one passage.

6. Convert the score to grade level.

Flesch Score	Grade Level
80–70%	7–8
70–60	9–10
60–50	11–12
50–40	13–15
40–30	16
30–20	college graduate

7. Identify the educational background of the audience.

8. Simplify vocabulary and style until the report's score matches the audience's average grade level. (According to Flesch, people actually like to read one grade lower than their capability.)

The invention of such complex formulas reminds us of the importance readability plays in information exchange. Simplicity and clarity are essential particularly in written communication where no possibility of immediate feedback exists. "Experience cannot be transmitted as *experience*"[8]; it must first be translated into linguistic symbols. Public administrators cannot communicate their thoughts without turning them into words—and they cannot communicate at all unless their words are understood.

5

Frame of Reference

Double agent Richard Sorge told Stalin that Hitler would attack the Soviet Union in 1941. Stalin shrugged off the warning. Before World War II, Vatican sources gave France the correct German army route through Belgium. French generals paid no attention.

Why did Stalin and the French military ignore vital information? It conflicted with their preconceptions. Stalin was certain that Hitler would not attack at that time. The French generals did not consider the Vatican's route militarily sound.[1]

One of the major problems in communicating is that people receive messages in an ongoing environment. Everyone has a unique way of looking at things, a personal *frame of reference*, that influences how he reacts to communications.

When a message corresponds with established beliefs, audiences focus on it avidly. They seek additional information and remember what they read or hear. However, information that conflicts with established beliefs is unpleasant to digest and recall. In this situation, members of the intended audience ignore, distort, or forget the message—as quickly as they can.

This reaction creates problems for the public agency manager, particularly in times of conflict and change. Administrators may ignore memoranda on innovative (but unpopular) processes; employees may distort or forget rules that conflict with their conception of how the job should be done.

Managers need to know: (1) how the screening mechanisms work (how employees avoid, modify, or forget information that upsets their equilibrium), and (2) how they, as leaders and communicators, can decrease the impact of frame-of-reference screening.

How Communications Are Screened

The three screening devices are selective exposure, perception, and retention.[2] Let us examine each in turn.

Selective Exposure

Making contact with an audience is an obvious precondition for communication. No matter how well you write, your message can have no impact unless it reaches its target. Yet many messages are simply ignored. People are subject to innumerable chats, letters, reports, and papers during their working lives, thus it is impossible for them to concentrate on all the data they receive.

Most of us throw out junk mail, sight unseen. The envelope is sufficient indication that the contents are uninteresting. Nobody buys all of the magazines that are available at the newsstand; each person examines a few that match particular needs and background.

The pattern of selective exposure continues in the agency. Administrators ignore messages they perceive as unimportant or hostile. Officials walk past bulletin boards, throw memoranda into the wastepaper basket, and file reports (without reading them) if they think the contents are inconsequential *for them.* Unfortunately, those who ignore a given message are generally those most in need of it. They tend to be ill-informed on the subject or antagonistic to the communicator's point of view.

The personnel administrator who considers deadlines superfluous is more than likely to disregard a list of "due dates" posted on a bulletin board. The forest ranger known for negligence in safety is a prime candidate to throw away the notice outlining new safety procedures. Too often agency messages reach administrators who are least in need of their contents.

Administrators ignore those communications they *think* have little payoff. But why do some messages appear unimportant? The fault may lie with the sender, the situation, or top management's values and traditions. Let us examine each cause.

The sender. Officials who swamp their staffs with written communications or send notices that are unreliable, outdated, or of poor physical quality ensure that some of their material goes unread. Too many managers send memoranda on every conceivable triviality. Their units have to pick and choose which to study. Since the junior administrator's interests are often different than the manager's, the unit may disregard precisely those notices that the manager considers essential. Important messages, then, drown in a sea of paper.

Other managers habitually send conflicting instructions. On Monday, they distribute one list of assignments. Come Tuesday, they rethink their plans. Eventually, the unit learns to disregard the first notice. Staff sit on their hands until they are certain of fixed responsibilities.

A third group of executives send (or post) schedules that become outdated shortly after they are received. Even when a particular schedule is accurate, seasoned administrators ignore it. Memoranda that are unattractively packaged or unnecessarily long also go unread.

The situation. Crises compel administrators to stop consulting handbooks and manuals; instant responses are the order of the day. Army Lieutenant Colonel Edward L. King (ret.) explains how the immediate pressures of war influenced junior American officers such as helicopter pilots in Vietnam: "They give you a big briefing book.... But no one really takes the time to read it—you're too busy trying to learn a new job."[3] King emphasizes that few people blame the officers for this. It is practically impossible to prepare for combat and study all the rules of command simultaneously. The problem is that the officers sometimes ignore rules that their superiors or political officials consider essential.

Top management's traditions and values. If top managers habitually disregard reports sent up the hierarchy, their subordinates may develop the complementary habit of ignoring notices meant for them. Too often top managers seize on plans and proposals that confirm their world view and ignore messages that challenge their preconceptions. They read reports prepared by "yes" men; file the others. As a result, administrators learn from leaders' behavior—as well as from their words. Selective exposure in high places implicitly encourages junior administrators to ignore controversial notices, too.

Selective Perception

A message read is not necessarily a message understood. A given agency communication rarely has the same meaning for the communicator and all potential recipients. First, individuals interpret messages in light of their own backgrounds and needs. People cannot tolerate meaningless information. They structure new messages by selecting, adding, deleting, and relating them to ideas they already know and value. They twist communications to fit their own world view.[4]

Second, in organizations the attitudes of informal groups affect perception. The human need to conform is strong enough so that administrators often change their interpretations to go along with a group consensus.[5] In order to get ideas across, the manager has to get a message past the individual's *internal* and the group's *social* filtering mechanisms.

Administrators tend to distort communications they *think* are irrelevant or harmful to them. What makes some legitimate messages appear trivial or threatening? Again, the cause may lie with the sender, the situation, or top management's traditions and values.

The sender. Managers invite selective perception when they frame messages without taking into account their audience's interests, values, and needs. For instance, in 1970 the new Detroit police commissioner wanted to encourage some two-way communication between the precinct inspectors and the central office. He framed a memorandum designed to elicit the inspectors' opinions on the causes of crime. The query, in part, read:

> I want you . . . to explain to the best of your ability, the reasons for increases or decreases in crime in your precinct, considering such factors as . . .
> • Population . . .
> • Income . . .
> • Unemployment. . . .[6]

The commissioner viewed the memorandum as a sympathetic attempt to relate to his staff. But the inspectors saw the query as a test of their own ability to prevent crime. Few analyzed the social reasons for crime increases; most simply got defensive and used the opportunity to argue for more officers, which was an economic impossibility.

The inspectors' backgrounds did not prepare them to contribute. In their experience, police commissioners were invariably authoritarian leaders, and they interpreted all queries in light of this preconception. Even when the commissioner tried to lead democratically, the inspectors misinterpreted his attempt.

The police commissioner invited selective perception by neglecting to analyze his audience's point of view and the preparation they needed to participate in policy making. Looking back on the incident seven years later, the commissioner admitted that he failed to relate.[7]

The situation. Crises increase the probability of distortion. When administrators are tense and overworked, almost any message can appear threatening. Rumors abound. The manager delivers one mild rebuke and the grapevine reports it as six dismissals. Insecure administrators then turn defensive. They rely on stereotypes to explain why the unit has problems. They become progressively less able to perceive the motives of others and the contents of their messages.

Top management's traditions and values. When high-level managers perceive selectively, they implicitly encourage junior staff to do the same. Distortion thus occurs both at high and low points on the hierarchy.

High-level officials also interpret messages based on their own preconceptions. A study of army officers in the 1950s shows that they habitually overestimated favorable attitudes of enlistees. The officers liked their work so they simply assumed the soldiers did also.[8]

The officers interpreted "sirs" and salutes as messages of genuine respect. However, the soldiers saw them as compulsory, outward signs of deference.

Most selective perception by top officials and their subordinates stems from an overreliance on one-way communications. Managers who rarely interact with staff tend to know little about their subordinates' interests. When they send messages down the chain of command, they cannot keep staff values in mind. When messages are sent to them, they lack adequate background to analyze them properly.

Selective Retention

Nobody remembers all of the information that he receives in a lifetime; we are all involved in a constant process of forgetting. (Quickly now: What color shoes did you wear on your third birthday? What is the title of the first poem you recited in school?)

Assume an administrator participates in a staff meeting. Immediately afterwards, every detail of the conversation is vivid in her mind. However, in the next few days, she undergoes a period of rapid forgetting, followed by a more gradual decrease in retention. Soon she remembers (at best) a few highlights. Studies show that organizational employees remember about fifty to sixty percent of the information they receive on the job.[9]

At least on a conscious level, administrators tend to remember messages that have pleasant connotations. They *repress* (or submerge into the subconscious) information that seems unpleasant, confusing, or contrary to their preconceptions. Lieutenant Colonel Edward L. King (ret.) estimates that only five officers out of a hundred remembered the army's confusing rules of land warfare in Vietnam.[10]

Sometimes managers give a difficult and threatening assignment, then wait a week and ask, "Where's the report?" The administrator replies, "I forgot all about it." The manager assumes he is lying. However, it is more than likely that the subordinate did forget an unpleasant assignment that he only heard about once.

HOW TO MINIMIZE SCREENING

Perfect understanding between managers and subordinates is impossible. There is always a gap between the information that the manager wants to convey and the information that the unit receives.

No manager can eliminate this gap completely, partly because some of it may be due to the situation or the actions of other people in the agency. However, all managers can take steps to keep the gap small, a crevice rather than a crater. Certain styles of initiation reduce selective exposure, perception and retention.

Reducing Selective Exposure

The manager's first task is to get the audience's attention. How well he succeeds depends to a large extent on four attributes of his messages: channels, frequency, reliability, and physical appearance.

Channels. In chapter 1, we explained why it is relatively easy to avoid written communications and much harder to ignore a face-to-face chat. When agency managers suspect that their units will ignore a notice on a controversial subject, they should speak to the staff personally, wherever possible. Once they get their unit's attention, they can follow up with a written message, after first alerting the unit to its importance.

Frequency. Effective initiators monitor how many messages they send. It is a common fallacy to assume that a greater number of messages means increased exchange of information. Actually, useless communications overwhelm an audience's receptive abilities. Crucial points get lost in an avalanche of trivia.

How does a manager know how many messages to send? Of course, there is no magic number that covers all contingencies. Officials use two-way communication to learn how much information their units are capable of assimilating; then they provide them with this amount of information, no less and no more.

Reliability. Reliable communicators try not to announce schedules (or other plans) prematurely. They wait until they have enough information to achieve accuracy.

Physical Appearance. Written communications should be as physically attractive as possible. People prefer memoranda with short paragraphs; try to limit most of yours to three or four sentences. Wide margins and the use of headings to demarcate sections also give a paper physical appeal.

Although people should not judge a book by its cover, they often do. A few minutes' attention to the details of presentation can increase the communicator's actual audience immensely.

Reducing Selective Perception

Assume an agency plans to install electronic data processing (EDP) equipment in two branches. One branch has recently suffered transfers and relocations of personnel because of previous technological installations. Administrators are fearful that the new equipment means further disruptions of social routines.

Here is a classic opening for selective perception. We know that people tend to hear what they expect to hear. Branch administrators expect the equipment to break up the unit; now they await confirmation of their fears.

What can the manager do? The worst move is to ignore the situation. The unit's grapevine can (and probably will) twist any noncommittal message the manager sends into "bad" news. Instead, the manager must be aware of the group's apprehensions and willing to confront them. Staff fears can be dealt with by tailoring messages to take into account each unit's perception of the circumstance.

To deflect specific fears the manager has to deal explicitly with the issue of transfers and relocations. Depending on the true state of events, he issues reassurances or identifies exactly the amount of disruption the change brings. Once this is out in the open, the chance of distortion is minimal.

How do managers become alert to staff fears in the first place?

The key is extensive vertical interaction with information flowing up and down the hierarchy. As we noted in chapter 2, extensive two-way communication fosters the manager's empathy with the unit. By interacting with staff, managers come to understand the reasons for their actions. Thus, they can take these reasons into account in sending messages to and decoding communications from the unit.

Meetings. Staff meetings are an excellent device for generating interaction.[11] Since managers get immediate feedback on controversial proposals, they can correct distortions as soon as they arise. Even when staff are ostensibly silent, managers often receive ample feedback from nonverbal cues—the raised eyebrow, slumping posture, or sneer that may be signs of unenthusiasm or anger. Alert communicators then ask themselves:

1. Why does the message inspire boredom or defiance?
2. What do I mean to communicate?
3. What am I actually saying to my audience?
4. How can I eliminate the difference?

In the section on "How Communications Are Screened," we described how Detroit's new police commissioner failed to communicate effectively with his staff. The cause of the problem was lack of empathy between the commissioner and the precinct inspectors.

If the police commissioner had called a staff meeting, he would have realized how uneasy democratic leadership made his subordinates. Armed with this knowledge, he would not have sent a memorandum, which is too cold and formal a device for introducing such a psychologically upsetting change. Instead, he might have discussed his plans in an informal atmosphere specifically designed to allay the inspectors' fears.

Timing. Meetings should be called relatively soon after an issue surfaces. Misperceptions are easiest to correct before people invest time and energy defending them.

Honesty. Effective managers never lie to staff or erase fears that are justified. Unpleasant duties do crop up in the public service; policy revisions can mean unpopular realignments of schedules and activities. A unit soon learns to discount all of a manager's reassurances if utopian promises are made that cannot be delivered.

Geographical Distance. Some staff are dispersed over too wide a geographical area to attend frequent meetings. In such cases, a letter requesting feedback makes a partial (if imperfect) substitute.

Headquarters officials of the U.S. Forest Service often need feedback from field personnel stationed all over the country. They mail the relevant documents to the reserves, with a note saying: "As usual, we wish, of course, to check with you and have your advice on these—and any other related problems—before making specific recommendations to higher authority."[12]

Forest managers realize that field officers have different perspectives from headquarters staff. Feedback from the reserves lets Washington-based officials see the gap between the meaning they want to communicate and that which they actually convey. Armed with this knowledge, they can initiate correspondence to bridge the gap.

Reducing Selective Retention

The key to reducing selective retention is the use of written communication. While face-to-face contacts reduce selective exposure and perception, they place a burden on the recipient's ability to recall.

In stress-laden situations, it is best for managers to initiate contact orally (wherever possible). However, after they receive feedback and clarify the agency's position, communicators should dispatch a written notice that: (1) reminds the administrators of the conversation; (2) stresses its importance; and (3) serves as a reference document.

Such notices should be kept short, clear, and easily comprehensible. Since message "overload" produces selective exposure, a long message is warranted only when conversations have genuine importance or contain particular details (e.g., dates, form numbers) that are difficult to recall. This two-step approach (oral initiation and written follow-through) has its greatest value in a rapidly changing environment where the norm is flux and innovation.

Fortunately, the processes of reducing selective exposure, perception and retention are closely related. All hinge, to a large extent, on understanding a particular audience's frame of reference, its unique way of perceiving and organizing oral and written messages.

In this chapter, we have identified the general relationship between background, values and needs, and various administrators' perceptions of agency messages. The next two chapters amplify this discussion by exploring in greater detail the influence two specific attributes—status and geographic distance—have on blockages and misunderstandings.

6
Status Differences

In chapter 1 we indicated that agency communications may be vertical, moving up and down the hierarchy, or horizontal between peers. Most misperceptions occur in vertical communications because people with different rank rarely share a common perspective; they each have "their own agendas."[1]

The agency head focuses on organizational goals, the bureau chief on unit objectives, the administrative analyst on completing a discrete project. Information that seems important to one often appears trivial to the others. As New York City's deputy mayor, John Zucotti, puts it, you can tell a person with limited responsibilities to cut a budget, but his "idea of where to cut may not be the same as yours."[2] Or as Miles' Law states, "Where you stand depends on where you sit."[3]

The effect of status differences on information exchange is worth extensive scrutiny because effective vertical communication is the lifeblood of public agencies. Every manager has a stake in understanding the mechanics of status distortion and the strategies for its reduction. (Officials want to transmit their messages to subordinates accurately and to receive "true" accounts in return.) Since the goal concept is central for understanding how status distortion operates, the first section begins with an analysis of organizational and personal goals.

How Status Distortion Operates

Stated and hidden goals abound in agencies. Each organization has a legislatively mandated goal that serves as its *raison d'etre;* this goal is broken into short and long range objectives for each program and unit.

Similarly, administrators bring a set of conscious and unconscious goals to their positions. These personal goals are partly bound up with the agency's mission and partly tied to social and career desires (which may or may not be useful for the bureau).

Goals and Communication

Personal goals affect communication because information does not transmit itself. Administrators who obtain certain information have to decide whether to share it with others. Naturally, in doing so, they ponder the consequences that transmission has for them. If they think the act furthers their own goals, they share the information; if they think transmission is disadvantageous, they may suppress it.

The decision to transmit information is personal, subjective, and idiosyncratic. For example, bureau chief Molly Smith thinks a delay in receiving certain forms is detrimental; she sends word of the bottleneck to her superior. Bureau chief Bob Vlahakis considers the exact same delay trivial; he does not report it.

Usually the tendency is to transmit "good" news, to suppress word of problems and failures. Administrators often perceive personal payoffs in publicizing their successes to superiors and subordinates. However, they believe they hurt their career and their social standing if they acknowledge problems to anyone except peers. The result is that "good" news flows freely up and down the hierarchy while word of incipient problems remains trapped at one level.

Downs argues that administrators only send unpleasant messages up the hierarchy if they think: (1) the boss will receive the news from some other channel (and it is better to tell him first), or (2) the boss needs the information to communicate with his own superior and will be displeased if he is caught without it.[4]

Top managers use similar "logic" in sending information *down*. Anyone who has seen an internal agency newsletter, house organ, or bulletin board knows that high officials exaggerate their triumphs, even when this means providing a lopsided view.

Such double-distortion (flowing up *and* down the hierarchy) has three negative consequences: superiors and subordinates (1) waste time covering up, (2) develop mutual distrust, and (3) fail to receive all the information they need.

The problem is compounded by the size of modern agencies. Most messages pass through several hierarchical layers before reaching their final audience. Since distortion can occur at each of these levels, a communication often changes radically during its vertical journey. The next subsection explains how this process of chain distortion works.

Chain Distortion

Chain distortion operates on messages sent up and down the hierarchy.[5]

Upward Bound. Distortion of upward-bound information is cumulative. Assume an agency has five layers of authority (see figure 6.1). An administrator at the E level sends a message to his superior, D_1. This official screens it and passes on the parts she considers important to C_1 who, in turn, reviews the message and sends part to B_1 and so on up the ladder. Four screenings occur before the information reaches A.

Two things happen during the screening process. First, each review condenses the information; every official only passes on part of the data received. This reduction is necessary, however; otherwise, the top official would be swamped with papers. But it means that the head of the agency (or even a unit) never gets to see most of the information the staff gathers.

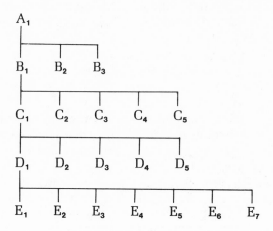

FIG. 6.1. MODEL OF AN AGENCY CHAIN

Second, the content of the information changes. Almost all reviewers play down problems that reflect badly on them and exaggerate triumphs that further their own personal and career goals. Thus, the top official receives a message that contains multiple errors and useless posturing (from his point of view).

Consider a revealing case involving combat effectiveness.[6] The army measures certain types of aircraft capability by radar bombing scores. For personal reasons, each bombardier is motivated to get the highest score possible and some cheat in preparing their reports. Squadron commanders generally know when cheating occurs. But each squadron commander is motivated to show that his unit outperforms the others. Thus they let the bombardier's reports stand—and sometimes add a bit of exaggeration on their own before sending the papers to the wing commander.

Being no fool, the wing leader realizes that the news is too good to be true. Still, he knows that airplanes are competing for Congressional funding with other offensive weapons and that the prestige of his section requires glowing reports. He accepts the data he receives, minimizing a few qualifying facts such as the number of air aborts, and sends the papers to top army officials.

The final audience receives a glowing report that grossly misinterprets reality. Army brass cannot plan adequately; they lack a data base for comparing weapon effectiveness. Such chain distortion impairs the agency's ability to function.

Downward Bound. Distortion of downward-bound information is also cumulative. Agency heads rarely give orders personally to "street-level" workers.[7] They transmit their directives to assistants who relay them to the unit chiefs who, in turn, send them still further down the hierarchy. Too often commissioners assume that the messages they intend to convey actually reach street-level administrators. However, matters are rarely that simple.

Let us return to figure 6.1. Assume A issues an order; it is most likely broad and generic.[8] B_1's task is to translate the order into more specific terms and send it to the C level. There, C administrators make it more specific still, send it to the Ds and so on down the chain of command.

For example, A says, "Cut costs." B_1 translates, "Cut operating costs. Do not interfere with safety procedures or client contact." C_2 amplifies, "Establish procedures to cut the operating costs relating to long-distance telephone use, replacement of equipment, and expense accounts."

The process of translation is rarely automatic. At each stage, administrators have a number of alternatives for amplifying a given order. Each official possesses some leeway in translating generic policy into specific rules and procedures.

But the amplification a given administrator chooses always reflects personal goals. Since the goals of A, B, C, and D are rarely (if ever) identical, it is highly unlikely that subordinates will pass on precisely the instructions A intended.

Perhaps B_1 believes a slight distortion of A's order will benefit him personally. Perhaps he believes it will benefit his unit. Perhaps he thinks that A's order is too difficult and must be modified in order to be implemented. Perhaps he is not even conscious of causing distortion, but he uses different language and emphasis than A and accidentally alters the chief's intentions.

In all these cases, the purpose A had in mind is shifted in

transmission. Each relayer changes the contents and the impact of the message.

Of course, A has the authority to check on subordinate performance and correct any errors. But A's time is limited. In actuality, only a few transmissions can be monitored. As a commentator on Franklin D. Roosevelt's cabinet notes:

> Half of a President's suggestions, which theoretically carry the weight of orders, can be safely forgotten by a Cabinet member . . . only occasionally, except about the most important matters, do Presidents ever get around to asking. . . .[9]

The norm is for policy to change as it moves down the hierarchy. As Downs observes, "In any large, multilevel bureau, a very significant portion of all the activity carried out is completely unrelated to . . . the goals of its topmost officials."[10]

Downward chain distortion impairs coordination of bureau policy. It hampers the topmost managers' ability to direct all unit activities towards achieving one overall, legislatively mandated goal.

While every agency has some problems with vertical communication, a number of steps exist for weakening chain distortion. The next section analyzes strategies for getting more accurate information from subordinates and checking on the fate of generic policies (relating the results at street-level with top management's intentions).

HURDLING THE STATUS BARRIER

How can a manager encourage subordinates to share unpleasant information? Strategies include using appropriate leadership style, eliminating middlemen, duplicating reports, and establishing statistical controls.

The Role of Leadership Style

Anderson suggests that there are four prerequisites to honest dialogue between manager A and a subordinate B. In regard to particular information, B must realize that: (1) it is important to A; (2) A does not already possess it; (3) an opportunity exists for transmittal; and (4) the odds of being hurt personally by exchange are low.[11]

Democratic leading helps managers meet the first three prerequisites. Through ongoing two-way communication, they keep the unit posted on the information they have and the data they need. By scheduling extensive opportunities for communication, they encourage subordinates to supply them with data. The manager's need for reliable information presents another good reason for introducing democratic leadership and involving the unit in decision making.

Anderson's fourth condition requires a climate free of excessive fear, a work environment where administrators are not ridiculed or demeaned for any slight mistake.

Generally, subordinates receive disapproval when they relate bad news. This happens because the recipients confuse their feelings about the news itself with their feelings about the exchange of information. While managers are sorry that a problem exists, they should be happy that a subordinate has confidence to inform them. A scowl is not the best way to encourage the employee to return. But *positive strokes* are.[12]

A *stroke* is any tactic one person uses to motivate another. Discipline and punishment are negative strokes; people try to avoid them. Words of appreciation are positive strokes; people seek them and some are highly prized.

Managers encourage administrators to communicate freely by rewarding those who do with positive strokes, including:

1. Showing interest in the communication.

2. Listening without interruption.

3. Thanking the communicator.

4. Involving the communicator in decision making to solve the problem.

5. Implementing positive action designed by the communicator.

6. Publicizing the communicator's role in planning a solution.[13]

Employees communicate freely when they perceive it is in their best interest to do so. The manager's motivational style influences whether administrators think they gain or lose by full, unbiassed exchange of information. As Downs notes, "Leaders who really do not like 'yes-men' usually do not get them."[14] The 'yes-man' goes where he is wanted.

Eliminating Middlemen

Top officials also reduce chain distortion by bypassing mid-level administrators whose role is to relay messages. By eliminating middlemen, initiators exchange information directly with bureaucrats far below them in the hierarchy—either to obtain data directly from those who gather it or to transmit orders directly to those who carry them out.

Let us look again at figure 6.1. A bypass occurs if A, B, or C transmits or receives information directly from administrators at the E level. The subsections below discuss four techniques frequently used to bypass the middleman. Three involve personal action by individual managers; the last is an organizational response. Each has its own advantages and disadvantages, making it appropriate for some—but certainly not all—agency situations.

The open door. The simplest bypass technique is the open door whereby agencies give employees the privilege of walking into any manager's office to discuss problems. The open door has two advantages. First, it has face validity: it seems like a good idea. Second, it can be implemented with relative ease; all top managers have to do is issue appropriate memoranda.

In practice, however, few subordinates take advantage of open doors even when high officials are available.[15] Habits die hard. Moreover, junior administrators know instinctively that their immediate supervisors resent the bypass. Subordinates risk a great deal by taking problems over their own boss's head; thus they generally remain silent even if they have information to convey.

Initiating contacts. Top officials usually get a better response initiating contacts rather than waiting for junior administrators to see them. Street-level employees are always surprised and often flattered by high-level visits, putting them in a receptive mood for exchanging information.

A former environmental protection commissioner in New York City gained a reputation for efficient management by initiating contacts with sanitation workers and getting information directly from them. Jerome Kretchmer felt that his immediate subordinates minimized the problems in the Sanitation Department, one of several agencies under his command. Unable to break through their cover-ups and distortions, he decided to seek data from the street-level employees.

In the early morning Kretchmer drove to a car barn where sanitation workers assemble. His presence electrified the workers who had simply assumed that commissioners never left their clean, heated offices. When the commissioner asked about complaints, the workers bombarded him with problems. The atmosphere was free and uninhibited, similar to the mood that prevails when friends exchange information. Kretchmer did not have to shout his desire for an honest view. His presence in the car barn was proof of his interest and sincerity.

Initiating contacts is a productive technique—in moderation. Frequent use causes a sharp drop in morale among the officials who are being bypassed. It indicates to them (and to their subordinates) that top management does not trust their ability to translate policy or report on day-to-day events. Used over a protracted time period, visits to the car barn would eventually undermine the leadership position of mid-level bureaucrats and create tension between them and their own subordinates.

Briefing sessions.   A third type of bypass involves the use of simultaneous briefing sessions. The aim here is for top officials to inform several layers of the hierarchy simultaneously about new policy. This strategy eliminates the middleman's role in downward communication, increases street-level morale, and is not as frightening to supervisors as direct, personal contact between top and bottom layers.

Top managers have neither time nor office space to hold many such sessions. And multilevel meetings are inappropriate for encouraging upward communication. Few employees will contradict a supervisor who is standing two steps away from them.

Flattening the hierarchy.   A final bypass strategy is to reduce the number of middlemen by changing the agency's structure. Organization theorists classify hierarchies as tall or flat. A tall hierarchy has many levels; a flat one has few (see figure 6.2).

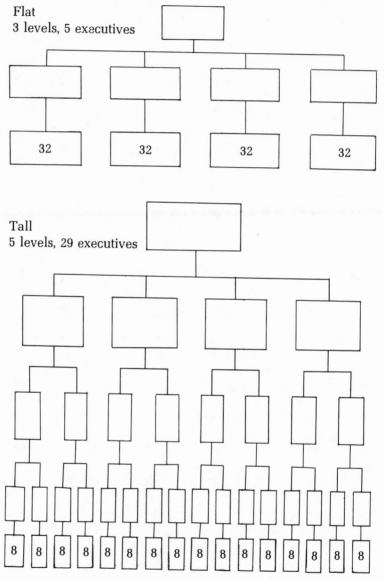

Flat
3 levels, 5 executives

32   32   32   32

Tall
5 levels, 29 executives

8 8 8 8 8 8 8 8 8 8 8 8 8 8 8 8

FIG. 6.2. HIERARCHIES AND SPAN OF CONTROL

Flattening the hierarchy reduces the number of screenings in upward and downward communication, thus keeping the amount of chain distortion relatively small.

Flat hierarchies lead to large spans of control where each manager has to supervise a relatively large number of people. (In figure 6.2, both hierarchies have 128 entry-level employees. The first-line managers in the flat hierarchy each supervise thirty-two administrators; their counterparts in the tall hierarchy each supervise eight.)

A question exists as to the impact wide spans of control have on agency performance. Twenty-five years ago, many organization theorists believed that a supervisor always had to monitor subordinates closely. Since there is a limit to the number of people a supervisor can control, the theorists advocated narrow spans.[16]

Today, theorists tend to argue that general supervision aids morale and often furthers productivity (see chapter 3). According to this view, wide spans have a unique advantage because they force managers to delegate responsibility. A manager with three subordinates can breathe down their necks, monitor their every move, and destroy all morale. An official with twenty immediate subordinates must practice more general supervision.[17]

Optimal span of control varies with an agency's goals. But an increase in general supervision is an unexpected bonus most agencies can receive if they flatten their hierarchies to reduce status distortion.

Duplicating Reports

A third strategy for reducing upward distortion is to establish dual communication channels for information exchange. If managers receive two reports on the same topic, they can check the accuracy of both. The subsections below discuss the advantages and disadvantages of two frequently used techniques of duplication: establishing overlapping responsibilities and the use of personal advisors.

Overlapping responsibilities. One technique for duplicating reports is to make several administrators responsible for the same function. Each then knows that any distortion in a report can be exposed by the others. Even if the boss does not know which account is true, the presence of disagreement leads to investigation.

A former administrator of the Boston Redevelopment Authority (BRA), Edward J. Logue, used this technique successfully in the 1960s. First, he appointed project directors to head BRA programs in the field; each director was told to report on problems. Then Logue appointed department heads who worked in the central office. They had overlapping responsibilities with the project directors. When the reports of a project director and a department head differed, the discrepancy always came to Logue's attention. Then he could call both administrators into his office and ferret out the true situation. As one project director commented, "the secret to Logue's success was the way in which he organized the BRA."[18]

Dysfunctions of overlapping responsibilities.   Creating overlapping responsibilities has costs as well as benefits. The most obvious cost is economic. The agency pays two people to perform one job—or, at least, to perform two jobs with built-in redundancies. Management can justify this only in terms of impressive communication benefits.

A more subtle cost is psychological. Overlapping responsibilities can produce resentment on the part of the administrators involved; this leads to tension, backbiting, and an unhealthy climate of fear and distrust.

If managers establish overlapping positions, they have a responsibility to maintain good rapport with both sets of administrators—and probably some mode of communication between them. Logue had this kind of rapport. As one BRA employee explained, "If I sent a memo . . . I always got a prompt answer. If I had a problem, I could just walk into his office and discuss it."[19] Without this supportive atmosphere, Logue's gains in communication might have been offset by massive losses in trust and motivation.

Personal advisors.   Another duplication technique is to seek additional information on a project from administrators who are not responsible for carrying it out. The rationale behind this strategy is that people who are responsible for implementing a project will not admit their own failures. An unbiassed account is most likely to come from administrators who have no ties to the group working on the project. But the question is: Where will the manager find administrators with knowledge to report but no operational responsibilities?

Every agency hires two types of administrators, *line* officials who carry out the organization's goal-directed activities and *staff* who perform support functions for the line. (For example, in a police department, detectives and patrol officers are line. Administrators who work in the personnel, legal, research, and training divisions are staff.)

Personal advisors to top officials are one component of an agency's staff. These advisors have no operating responsibilities. Their only function is to help top management make effective decisions by collecting and assessing information and providing adequate technical advice.

Advisors break the line's monopoly on communication. They give the top executive a better picture of agency performance.

The need for nonline communication was one reason President Carter abolished the Domestic Council as an advisory body and replaced it with the Domestic Policy Staff. Presidents Nixon and Ford relied for advice on a Domestic Council composed of the various cabinet secretaries with national program responsibilities. Since each of these officials had his own domain to protect, the advice they gave was often tinged with institutional biases. President Nixon found this advice so distorted that he almost never called council meetings.

When President Carter assumed office, he abolished the council. Knowing that line officials often protect their own units, he preferred to rely on a Domestic Policy Staff, directed by a personal advisor who had no ties to any cabinet department.[20]

Dysfunctions of personal advisors. The psychological problem with the use of advisors is similar to that associated with overlapping jobs. Tension develops between line and staff. Line administrators often view staff as intruders, people who can afford to criticize because they never have to perform.

The line often believes that staff are too far removed from

day-to-day activities to really understand operating problems.
For example, a social caseworker may feel that advisors at
headquarters cannot understand the realities of client contact. A
principal may believe that the board of education's legal advisors
cannot fathom the need to suspend unruly pupils.

Thus, line officials resent when top management changes
policy based on the recommendation of personal advisors. After
all, it is the line that bears the brunt of any change in work
routine.

Again, only democratic leading and extensive two-way
communication can relieve this kind of tension. Managers must
stress the *advisory* nature of staff work, solicit input from the line
on staff suggestions, and involve the line in decision making (at
least to the extent they involve staff).

A more subtle problem relates to the loyalty of personal
advisors. In large agencies, advisory staffs grow so large that they
generate hierarchies of their own. Personal assistants report to
personal associates rather than directly to top managers. In this
climate, the staff's loyalty to the chief executive is diluted;
personal advisors develop allegiances to their own cause. They
withhold information that reflects badly on past advice and
emphasize communications that expand their own role (e.g., the
need for more research before making decisions).

But advisors reduce distortion even when they have their own
loyalties. The function of staff is to serve as a second
communication channel. Managers who have many personal
advisors really supervise two hierarchies, staff and line. They can
use the information they receive from one to check up on the
other (even if neither is free from bias).

The possibility of collusion between line and staff is small
because their interests differ. To justify their existence, advisors
have to criticize the line's performance and offer suggestions for
change. The evidence of problems that line officers seek to bury
is precisely the information that staff advisors are paid to find.
The conflict between line and staff is inherent in the nature of
the work each does. Tensions generated by this conflict ensure
that top managers gain when they rely on reports prepared by
both sets of administrators.

Using Statistical Controls

A fourth strategy for reducing distortion is to develop objective measures of performance and require that subordinates include them in reports. Since figures are generally considered hard to distort, managers often insist on receiving a constant flow of statistics. How many felony arrests per precinct? How much loss of life by fire per year? How many ineligibles stricken from the welfare rolls this quarter?

This type of information enables agency executives to monitor performance and plan for the future. In some situations, it also helps managers practice general supervision; they can evaluate results rather than the details of subordinate performance.

Selecting measures. The first problem associated with statistical controls is the difficulty of choosing appropriate measures. Selection should be a joint activity of managers and subordinates where they explicitly (1) identify the unit's goals; (2) translate them into measurable indicators; and (3) establish data collection procedures. For example, the goal of an urban transportation program might be to "provide access to community services, facilities, and employment in a safe, quick, comfortable ... manner."[21] As it stands, this goal cannot be measured; no procedures exist for direct quantification of safety or comfort. In order to measure these concepts, we must first translate them into quantifiable criteria. A particular urban transportation analyst might translate them as follows:

1. for safety, the rate of transportation-related death, injury and property damage;

2. for speed, the time required to travel between preselected origin and destination points;

3. for comfort, the bumpiness of the road surface.[22]

Manager and unit must then agree on what constitutes acceptable performance and propose procedures for collecting evidence.

Disagreement can arise at almost any stage of this process. For example, administrators might argue whether to include property damage in a safety index; some might like to restrict it to personal death and injury. Differences can arise over what constitutes acceptably quick service. How long should it take a bus to go from Avenue A to 134th Street? One hour? Fifty minutes? Forty-five? Of course, managers can impose answers by fiat. But group participation yields valuable insights and increases member allegiance to quantified reports.

The limits of statistical measures.   Even with group participation, there are limits to the type of information that statistics can provide. Much of the data public managers need simply eludes quantification. At best, statistical reporting gives public managers a clearer perspective on part of their terrain.

A sharp distinction can be drawn between the use of statistical controls in business and in the public sector. Private corporations exist to make a profit. When employees measure production, sales, or costs, the company gets information that relates directly to its overall goal.

Public agencies, on the other hand, sometimes have goals that are so intangible that it is extremely difficult to find techniques for measuring them. What criteria do we use to measure whether an agency "increases justice" or "improves interracial harmony"? Yet these are important public objectives.

Most agencies embrace some functions that can be measured quantitatively and others that cannot. In these organizations, emphasizing statistical reports actually distorts the flow of communication because administrators concentrate excessively on reporting the activities they can quantify. Eventually this distortion in communication results in lopsided behavior; activities that are not reported seem less important than those that are.

For instance, fire departments are created to prevent and control fires. We can measure firefighting activities by a number of quantitative indexes (e.g., hours pumped, lines laid, ladders hoisted, etc.), but it is difficult to quantify fire prevention. Accordingly, the annual reports of big-city fire departments concentrate on the firefighting side of the job. Pages are devoted to assessing time spent controlling blazes while no attempt is made to evaluate time devoted to fire prevention. This leads to a situation where fire officers tend to think fighting fires is a more important part of their job than preventing them.[23] An agency that relies on statistical controls has to institute alternate communication routes for reporting on nonquantifiable functions.

Distorting statistics. The final problem with statistical controls lies with their actual vulnerability to distortion. The conventional wisdom claims numbers are distortion proof but evidence suggests that administrators often doctor numbers rather than report poor performance.

For example, sanitation agencies measure performance by weighing tons of garbage collected per truck per shift. In New York, sanitation workers respond by stopping at the firehouse and getting their trucks squirted full of water.[24]

Education agencies often measure school performance by assessing students on standardized examinations. In these districts, teachers have been known to give students copies of the exams in advance in order to increase their scores.

Administrators may tamper with numerical evidence if they perceive that it is in their own personal interest to do so (and there is little danger of their being caught). The only way to prevent this is by involving entire units in selecting measures and maintaining an atmosphere of mutual trust between manager and group. Otherwise, Downs' law of countercontrol comes into play:

> The greater the effort made by a ... top-level official to control the behavior of subordinate officials, the greater the efforts made by those subordinates to evade ... such control.[25]

CONCLUSIONS

As this chapter suggests, there is no *sure-fire* way to eliminate status barriers. In the final inning, the manager's last line of defense lies in personal awareness. Alert officials realize that the information they receive is sometimes distorted. They know that the phrase "I cannot tell the boss what I really think" is common enough in public agencies.[26] Astute managers maintain a healthy skepticism to news of messianic improvements. They remain alert to the way the personal goals of their superiors and subordinates affect information transmittal, and to the way their own goals may affect the information they send to others.

7

Geographical Distance

One of the most striking aspects of American public agencies is their geographical dispersion. Few federal, state, or local bureaus conduct all their business from one location.

Client-centered city agencies (e.g., schools, welfare, police) generally consist of a headquarters, located near the center of town, and field units. Top management and staff departments (accounting, personnel, research, etc.) work at headquarters. Street-level workers and their immediate supervisors are field personnel.

A similar pattern prevails in federal and state departments, although most do not provide direct client service. Again, top management and staff work at headquarters (in Washington, D.C., or the state capital) and the lower line occupies regional or field offices.

In order to communicate with colleagues, public managers must increasingly reach across great distances and coordinate units geographically separated. Take the case of James Webb,

administrator of the National Aeronautics and Space Administration (NASA). In order to coordinate the Apollo space program,
Webb had to keep in contact with his own staff at headquarters
in Washington, D.C., engineering personnel in Houston, Texas,
rocket builders in Huntsville, Alabama, and launching pad
officials in Cape Kennedy, Florida. This meant that he had to
transmit policy and accept information from hundreds of
administrators he could never meet or engage in face-to-face
conversation.

It is hard enough to communicate clearly with someone who
shares your office; but clues to understanding disappear rapidly
as the distance between communicator and audience grows. Like
status variance, geographical distance increases the likelihood of
distortion.

This chapter explores geographical bias from two points of
view. First, we analyze some of the reasons for two-way
distortion between field and headquarters. Second, we consider
strategies for improving communication across distance.

DISTORTION AND GEOGRAPHY

Misperceptions arise between headquarters and field personnel because of different regional perspectives, inadequate
communication techniques, and the time lag between initiation
and reception of messages. Let us examine each of these reasons.

Different Perspectives

Administrators' geographical locations affect their perspective
in the same way that status does. Culture and tradition vary with
geographical milieu, influencing the way in which bureaucrats
perceive public issues.

Regional culture.   Political scientist Daniel Elazar argues that
the United States has three geographically differentiated
cultures.[1] New England and parts of the Midwest are moralistic;
their administrators tend to view government as a positive
instrument to advance the general welfare. The Middle Atlantic
states and the older areas in the Midwest (Ohio, Indiana) are
individualistic. Their culture puts greater stress on the limits of

government and the importance of the private sector. The old South is *traditionalistic*. Politics and public administration are considered caretakers for the established interests. The West has pockets of moralistic, individualistic, and traditionalistic culture.

To the degree that Elazar's map reflects reality, administrators in each region have different goals and priorities. Federal policy made in Washington, D.C., is interpreted differently by field officers in the various regions.

Local culture. Elazar's theory accounts for only a fragment of the geographical variance in this country; actually, many cultures coexist in each region. State agencies find that priorities differ by county or local area (and, hence, enforcement of state statutes differs as well). City officials learn that each neighborhood takes pride in its unique flavor.

Issues that appear crucial at the headquarters of a state or city agency often seem trivial in certain districts and vice versa; bureaucratic strategies that make sense in one area appear irrelevant elsewhere. State auditors, teachers, social workers, police, and other street-level administrators frequently complain that officials in the central office are unaware of conditions in the field.

Some of the resulting tension is useful to agencies. Particularly in poor, inner-city neighborhoods, field officials can serve as conduits between the community and headquarters. If they find that clients are hostile to particular policies or procedures, they can report this and work to make the agency's programs more responsive to the needs of its clientele.[2] However, the differences in perspective between center and periphery also have disadvantages for agency performance.

A vicious cycle. Differences in perspective can lead to alienation when branch personnel feel cut off from the central office. An "us" versus "them" mentality develops; field officers give their primary loyalty to the local unit rather than to the agency as a whole. In this environment, they view centralized reporting requirements as so much snooping and thus conceal their branch's shortcomings from headquarters.

Recent studies of the Department of Health, Education and Welfare's Social and Rehabilitation Service (SRS) highlight the problem. Asked about the value of headquarters, regional administrators responded that they made most of their own decisions and that Washington was "not much help."[3] After the regional offices implemented a new operational planning system, central office staff did not provide any feedback (or even bother to call them). In turn, regional administrators did not reveal their problems to headquarters.[4]

When communication erodes between branch and center, headquarters becomes anxious about inadequate supervision. Forgetting that they lack information on branch conditions, headquarters staff tighten the reins unilaterally, thereby increasing the number of written directives and decreasing their tolerance for deviation. Eventually, distortion and defensiveness dominate all communication.

The Washington office of the U.S. Forest Service once ordered two rangers to rake up all the dead wood in the Lewis and Clark Reserve in Montana. Since this reserve contained three million acres, with dead trees larger than a city block, the rangers refused. The Washington office replied, "It is the duty of forest officers to obey their instructions and not to question them."[5]

Inadequate Techniques

The problem of perspective is exacerbated by the lack of face-to-face communication. People who work at a distance perforce forgo informal, personal, daily chats. They must rely on written correspondence or mechanical devices (usually the telephone). Face-to-face communication has unique advantages, particularly when the initiator and the audience have different frames of reference. Communicator and audience can interact holistically, employing body language and intuitive gestures. The give and take of informal conversation affords an opportunity to ask questions and cement understanding.

Daily personal contact stimulates communication.[6] When administrators meet every day, they exchange information as a social act. A lot of work-related conversation occurs over coffee, lunch, or mid-morning gossip. This type of casual communicating gives both initiator and audience pleasure—many officials hardly view it as work at all—yet it advances the agency's mission.

Writing is generally less socially satisfying than talking. In fact, many administrators find it difficult, time consuming, or tedious.

The telephone, while closer to face-to-face, is costly and lacks the warmth of personal interchange—a liability that is particularly apparent in conference calls where three or more people share the line. The lack of visual cues also minimizes the social pleasure of participants.

Because communicating at a distance is less satisfying, administrators often forgo information exchange until it is absolutely necessary. As a result, supervision suffers and useless duplication of function can ensue.

Time Lag

Historically, time lag was the principal barrier to inter-office communication. Prior to the invention of telegraph and telephone, messages travelled so slowly that it was impossible for branch staff to consult headquarters on a regular basis. Top officials had to let them make decisions on their own. The invention of the telephone eliminated most of the time lag barrier, increasing the central office's ability to control the field. In emergencies, geographically dispersed staff use the telephone to consult on an hour-by-hour basis.

Changes in diplomacy highlight this trend. Prior to our own century, America's ambassadors enjoyed great leeway in negotiating with foreign powers. (It was physically impossible for them to check constantly with the State Department.) Today diplomats have much less discretion than their nineteenth-century counterparts. They *can* (and therefore *must*) communicate with superiors in Washington.

Time lag remains a problem in nonemergency situations where center and field still communicate in writing, a process that can take several weeks (from initiation to reception). This residual time lag reinforces barriers to effective communication created by the almost inevitable differences in perspective between branch and center.

Assume, for example, that the Veterans Administration issues new medical procedures in January; clinics in outlying branches may not receive copies until February (or even March). Assume further that the Veterans Administration chief announces the new procedures at a televised press conference on January 1. The next morning, clients bombard the clinics with questions and branch staff must reluctantly confess that they have not yet received copies.[7] Is it any wonder that they feel alienated from headquarters? Lack of speedy, efficient, direct communication routes increases misunderstanding between geographically dispersed personnel.

HURDLING GEOGRAPHICAL BARRIERS

Any attempt to achieve effective communication over distance must take into account both the psychology and technology of information exchange. Agency managers need to unify perspectives between center and field. They also need to develop technologically innovative substitutes for personal contact and proximity, electronic systems that continue the revolution begun by the telegraph and telephone.

Unifying Perspectives

How can agencies create loyalty to themselves rather than to particular units? How can they expand administrators' horizons so that "each member of the management team ... can understand the meaning in the minds of other members"?[8]

Below we describe three strategies agencies use to develop empathy, the ability of field and center to put themselves in each other's shoes: prior education, in-career training, and rotation of field personnel. (The limitations of each strategy are also explored.)

Prior education.   Professionalized agencies instill loyalty by hiring branch and headquarter staff with similar backgrounds. Directives are then presented as professional prescriptions, resting on specialized knowledge that the center and branch share. The agency tags its procedures as the professionally sanctioned way of getting things done. Unity of perspective increases because center and field share a professional orientation.

However, overreliance on professionalization leads to an inbred bureau that often ignores innovative ideas proposed by outsiders (see chapter 2). It also may decrease the responsiveness of field workers to individual communities. Feeling a strong professional loyalty to the center, they may be less willing to take community preferences into account in planning policy.

In-career training. Another strategy is to give field and center unified in-career training. Agencies mix branch and headquarter personnel at two- to five-day interactive workshops where both groups get a chance to identify priorities.

It is difficult to understand the regional needs of people who work in another geographical area. Thus the training workshops introduce administrators to their counterparts in other offices, while affording an opportunity for holistic, satisfying face-to-face chats. Center and field finally get to speak to each other—even if only for a few days. Pent-up hostilities emerge; each group learns how its actions cause informational difficulty for the other. Unfortunately, finances place sharp limits on the number of workshops an agency can undertake. It is expensive to transport field workers to a central location, particularly in federal and state agencies.

Rotation. A third strategy is rotation of field personnel to prevent excessive identification with one region or neighborhood. The State Department rotates the diplomatic posts of Foreign Service Officers (FSOs), even assigning some to tours of duty in our own state and local governments. The Forest Service rotates rangers. Police departments routinely shift officers from one precinct to another.

A disadvantage of frequent rotation is that administrators cannot develop expertise in the problems of a given area. An FSO who spent twenty years in El Salvador would know quite a bit about its culture; a ranger who worked in one reserve for an entire career would have its layout and aesthetic beauties down pat.

Agencies often forgo geographic expertise in order to broaden the field staff's perspective. Knowledge of (and perhaps commitment to) a particular area takes a back seat to increasing the administrator's sense of identification with the whole organization. When an agency rotates, it increases empathy and co-ordination at the expense of geographic flexibility. That so many agencies are willing to make this trade suggests the importance of unifying the perspectives of branch and headquarters.

Innovations in Technique

Geographically dispersed organizations need mechanical substitutes for the proximity that yields undelayed flows of information. Many public agencies currently look to computers as a substitute for geographical homogeneity, using them to collect and store field-generated data.

Computerized systems are common in Washington and the federal government is currently investing considerable funds developing electronic data processing (EDP) systems for local governments. Between 1974 and 1979, the Urban Information Systems Inter-Agency Committee, a consortium of ten federal agencies, spent $26 million to help local governments build "comprehensive information systems."[9] The Law Enforcement Assistance Administration spent additional sums on police agency software; the Census Bureau developed EDP applications for urban planning departments. Two advantages of EDP systems are that they cut residual time lag and standardize reporting.

Cutting time lag. Computers perform information searches much more quickly than unaided administrators. Ten years ago it took Air Force commanders in Washington, D.C., a full three months to staff a task force to assist in diplomatic negotiations. (Headquarters needed a quarter of a year to find out which officers had the proper skills and where each officer was located.) Today the same search takes less than a week—thanks to an advanced data system.[10]

Standardizing reports. Assume a state agency allows regional branches to request funds on any form they devise. What happens? Twenty branches? Twenty forms! If a computerized budgetary form is designed, it imposes a standardized reporting language on all regional offices. The possibility of distortion is limited somewhat because all locations use one code.

The design of computerized reporting forms affords an excellent opportunity for joint decision making by managers at headquarters, field units, and EDP specialists. An appropriate division of responsibility might be:

1. Identify the need for computerized reporting forms (headquarters).

2. Ascertain the information that the central office needs from the field and that the branches can supply to the central office (headquarters, field units, and EDP specialists).

3. Construct alternative questionnaires or other devices for collecting this information (headquarters, field units, and EDP specialists).

4. Select the questionnaire or other device best suited to the data available (headquarters, field units, and EDP specialists).

5. Reduce the questionnaire or other device to mathematical form; devise a computer program to process it (EDP specialist).

6. Explore appropriate ways of using the output (headquarters with advice from the field units).[11]

This division requires the agency to maintain intricate communication networks that bridge geographical and functional boundaries. Extensive two-way communication between headquarters and field is a prerequisite; interactive workshops or conferences are needed.

In addition, problems may arise when line managers (whether headquarters or field) exchange information with EDP staff. Few line managers have the expertise to set up computer programs themselves but most may find they speak "a different language" from the EDP personnel. The line–staff interchange works best when program managers have some mathematical literacy (at least a college course in statistics or programming) and the EDP specialists refrain from using jargon or professionalized gobbledygook. Thus, the "best" use of innovative techniques tends to occur in agencies that have already overcome internal language barriers and made progress towards unifying perspectives.

Limitations. The limitations of computers are similar to those of statistical controls (see chapter 4). EDP systems are only useful in communicating data that can be expressed in mathematical terms. A lot of complex information on attitudes or morale simply cannot be conveyed by computer.

In the end, also, the worth of a computer depends on the ability of the manager who installs it. Like the typewriter, the computer is a tool. The machine collects and stores information from distant places but only the human being provides the judgment, initiative, and common sense that turn data into effective decisions.[12]

CONCLUSIONS

All agencies experience tension between the tendency towards centralized and decentralized administration. On the one hand, top management must control agency operations and see that they are in line with the legislative mandate. On the other hand, some geographical flexibility promotes a responsiveness to the community, a positive value.[13]

While writers on administration differ on how much central control is needed, all agree that top management must have an accurate, timely flow of information from the field. Yet the agency's fight to reduce geographical distortion is as difficult as the battle over status barriers. Again, there are no sure-fire techniques, although attempts to unify perspectives and install innovative equipment are useful in certain situations.

Ultimately, geographical barriers are only surmounted where empathy exists between center and field. Then, headquarters recognizes the need for continued flexibility in the face of community preferences and branch staff develop loyalty to the goals of the entire organization.

8
Time Limits

At one point or another almost all public administrators complain about time limits. Who has not said: "If only I had another week to finish that report." "If only they gave me another day to prepare that presentation." "If only I found time to research that point." The search for the twenty-five hour day is as endless as the quest for the Fountain of Youth—and as futile, because we already have all the time there is.

TIME PRESSURE

Time pressure is a recognized constraint in public agencies; at all levels, officials feel that their superiors make excessive demands on their time. For too many administrators work expands to fill the time available.[1] No matter how the significance or complexity of their tasks change, they always have to work every available minute in order to meet deadlines.

Faced with a workload they consider heavy, administrators often rush from task to task without setting priorities. For example, Arnold Packer, a former assistant secretary for policy at the Department of Labor, admits that he had an important conceptual idea about international economics and U.S. productivity while working in Washington, but found that "there just isn't the creative time to do it, partially because you are just too busy and even if you could put aside the time you are too fatigued."[2] Patricia Wald, former federal assistant attorney general for legislative affairs, found that she could not set her own schedule in the office, because she usually had to "go to whatever the crisis is."[3]

We know that communication is an indispensable agency activity. But, under pressure, administrators are likely to neglect it for two reasons. First, some communication procedures are inefficient. Managers may require overlong, extraneous reports. Staff meetings can degenerate into time-wasting forums if people report irrelevant successes to inflate their own egos. Second, some of the consequences of communication may be undesirable. If initiators fear certain information may be used against them, they may delay or withhold data.

When administrators experience unrealistic expectations and a climate unconducive to vertical exchange in some communication situations, they tend to overgeneralize and assume that communication itself is a waste of time. They assign it low priority and then wonder why decision making suffers.

Time Pressure and Decision Making

Time pressure affects an agency's decisions by limiting the search for information.[4] Four dysfunctional search-related consequences occur when decision makers feel pressed for time:

1. Officials consider only a few of the many available alternatives.

2. They give primary consideration to alternatives which represent an extension of the status quo rather than a significant change.

3. Stereotypes rear their ugly heads. Since judgment on an individual basis takes too long, decision makers rely on prefabricated categories.

4. Relatively few people participate in decision making.

Restrictions on communication prevent people from learning about the deliberations; there is no time to seek multiple perspectives.

The end result tends to be an excessively narrow decision-making process. Useful alternatives are not examined. The old is blindly preferred even when the new might be more efficient or equitable. Important frames of reference are ignored. If agencies want a thorough job of information search and analysis, they must train their officials to manage their time. The next section identifies representative strategies of time management with special emphasis on their use in improving communication.

TIME MANAGEMENT

Why do so many administrators feel ground under the heel of time? The problem can have external causes (e.g., the supervisor divides the work inequitably or retracts assignments). But more often it is internally generated—administrators simply waste the time they have.

A constant feeling of being rushed and overwhelmed generally arises from bad habits incurred from not knowing how to manage one's time in the first place. The solution requires self-development. Administrators must learn to set priorities and find the time for them; time-wasting habits must be identified, analyzed, and to the extent possible, replaced with more productive styles.

Managing one's time is similar to managing an agency program. Both activities improve with thought and practice. Both require planning, organization, and implementation.

Planning Time

Former HEW Secretary Joseph Califano kept a poster on his office wall with a quote from Thoreau: "It is not enough to be busy . . . the question is: what are we busy about?"[5]

The aim of planning time is to direct work efforts—in other words, to work less and accomplish more. One hour of planning can shorten "doing" by three or four hours and produce better results.

The first step in planning time is to list goals. For a given administrator, this means asking: Where do I want to be (in terms of agency work) in one year? half a year? three months?

As an exercise, write out your own personal goals for the month, using full sentences. By transferring thoughts to paper, you inadvertently make the goals more specific and concrete. (Some you may drop altogether as unrealistic or poorly conceived.) The completed list probably contains more goals than you have time to reach. So you must set priorities. Which goal is most crucial? Which is next? Goals can usually be arranged in a sequence of descending importance.

Next list the activities needed to reach each goal. When these include complex projects (e.g., writing a report), subdivide them into concrete tasks (e.g., outline, research, write section I). Then list the tasks and approximate the amount of time each requires. (When in doubt, always allow yourself more time than you think necessary. Remember Murphy's Law: If something can go wrong, it probably will.)

Pace your performance; indicate the starting and completion dates for every task. (Of course, they can overlap; you do not necessarily have to finish one task before starting another.) Check the list and make certain that each task actually contributes toward reaching the goal.

Now look at what you have: a long-range plan tailored to meeting your goals, the type of plan that any public administrator can convert into a daily schedule.

Organizing Time

An administrator needs two items in order to construct a schedule: the long-range plan and an appointment calendar. The last thing each evening, he checks the plan and calendar, identifying the tasks he wants to accomplish the next day. Then he schedules each task into a specific time slot, letting the nature of the tasks and his own biorhythms determine placement.

Activities that require concentration (e.g., research, writing) should be blocked into hours where there is relatively uninterrupted peace and quiet. Certain tasks (e.g., computer programming) may require use of equipment that is only available at specified times.

Everybody has certain hours of the day during which he or she is most alert. For some people, morning is a time of great invigoration; others do not perk up until noon. Administrators should schedule top priority projects for slots when their individual energy levels are high. They can do routine work—answer telephone calls, sign letters, keep up with professional reading—during low-energy periods.

While secretary of the Department of Housing and Urban Development, Patricia Harris insisted that her staff leave her alone for the first hour and a half in the morning. This was her fresh time, when she wanted to concentrate on top-priority matters and not be interrupted for less important business.[6]

Implementing the Schedule

Some administrators are excellent at writing schedules but poor at keeping them. It takes genuine willpower to proceed from task to task without procrastination. Here are several bad habits that slow officials down.

Leaving the job at hand. Despite a desire to tackle high-priority items, administrators sometimes lapse from the schedule. They chat with visitors, take frequent coffee breaks, accept unimportant telephone calls. Then they evince surprise when they cannot meet deadlines.

In order to break the habit of wasting time, the administrator must search for the root cause—within himself. Why does he seek interruptions? Is he bored? Is he frightened, secretly afraid that he cannot write a satisfactory report? Is he overtimid, unwilling to hurt a colleague's or visitor's feelings by ending a social conversation?

Once administrators identify the root cause, they can work to change their own attitudes. Rearranging the schedule or pursuing effective ten-minute relaxation breaks (e.g., through exercises or Yoga) can relieve boredom and enliven the senses. Specific planning can reduce fear. Any sensible person might shudder at the vague assignment, "Write a report." The task assumes manageable proportions when you list all its components; for example, identify sources of information and explore procedures for obtaining them.

Overtimidity in social encounters can be alleviated with some polite assertiveness. A telephone call can be declined or deferred pleasantly. A lengthy conversation may be averted with a short explanation at the onset: "Sorry, this can only be three minutes, Tom. Someone is waiting for instructions."

A few high-level officials use mechanical devices to overcome fears of interruptions. John McNaughton, assistant secretary of defense under Robert McNamara, used a miniature traffic light to protect himself from excessive intrusions. A red light meant that he did not want to be disturbed; a green light signalled that he was ready and willing to receive visitors.[7]

Searching for perfection. Another cause of time waste is the fruitless search for perfection. Given the assignment to write a second Bible or *Iliad*, who would not put off completion? But agency reports are functional documents. They do not have to elevate or entertain.

A fundamental administrative skill is knowing how to balance the need to secure adequate information and the need to produce it on time. Waiting for *all* the facts ensures that decisions will never be made because the information available to any one agency is always incomplete. Decisions are enacted under conditions of risk or uncertainty. At some point, the administrator must prepare the report, even if all the facts are not in. Effective performance requires action, closure, completion of assignments. When a task is particularly demanding, administrators can say to themselves, "Well, if I must do it, I'll start this way and do the best job I *can*."

Failing to delegate. A third cause of time waste is failure to delegate minor tasks to subordinates. Delegation should be a basic part of every agency official's administrative repertoire, yet some managers love details as their occupational hobby.

Those who refuse to delegate duties defend their conduct by saying: "How can I delegate? My staff lacks experience; the unit will make too many mistakes." Or, "If I pass it to a subordinate, I'll lose control." Or, "No one knows how I want the task done." Or, "Nobody else has time to do it. I better load it on my own shoulders."

Actually, delegation has benefits for both subordinates and

superiors. It exposes subordinates to new responsibilities, gives them on-the-job training, raises morale, and thus frees the manager to concentrate on more pressing concerns.

For delegation to be effective, the manager must make the following decisions:

1. *Choose a task that is suitable for delegation.* Generally, this means choosing a relatively routine activity that recurs. In order to find a suitable job, managers can ask themselves, "What minor decisions repeat themselves every day, week, or month? What job details take the largest chunk of my time?"

2. *Select an administrator who has the appropriate qualifications.* The manager identifies someone who has the background to complete the task successfully; who is interested in performing the task and will do so with enthusiasm; who can learn from the task in terms of long-range professional growth.

3. *Communicate the purpose and nature of the work.* Subordinates must be informed of expected standards and limitations on their authority. For example, does the delegation of a particular task mean they can

   a. take action, hence no further contact with the manager is needed;
   b. identify action only and wait for the manager's acquiescence; or
   c. look into the matter, present alternative actions and let the manager make the decision?

An explicit relationship should be established before the administrator starts working.

4. *Secure acceptance of the assignment.*

5. *Maintain effective relationship with the person to whom the task is delegated.* The manager provides encouragement when needed and clarifies misunderstandings.

6. *Be tolerant of minor errors.* No one can be right 100 percent of the time. Subordinates may not complete the task exactly as the manager would have done; but if the results and timing are acceptable, does it really matter?

A well-developed ability to delegate responsibility helped earn Carla Anderson Hills, former secretary of HUD, a reputation for professional speed and decisive administration. A deputy assistant secretary recalled a time when Ms. Hills accepted his own appraisals of a package of materials and signed the papers on the basis of that trust. In this way, a minimum of time was lost, the assistant's responsibility was confirmed, and Carla Hills could turn to matters which demanded her full attention.[8]

Conclusions

The waste of valuable work time is a serious problem in public agencies. One management consultant hypothesizes that officials (in general) spend eighty percent of their time on trivialities, only twenty percent on top-priority problems.[9] Parkinson's Law of Triviality states: "The time spent on any item of the agenda will be in inverse proportion to the sum involved."[10] Administrators must learn to manage their time by planning and organizing a schedule and then sticking to it as much as possible.

The next two units explore strategies for communicating effectively in various situations in a public agency. The ability to schedule one's time is a prerequisite for putting into practice any of these strategies.

Summing Up
Concepts for Review;
Problems and Exercises

113

Headquarters and field
Regional culture
  individualistic
  moralistic
  traditionalistic
Electronic data processing
Time management
Delegation

PROBLEMS AND EXERCISES

1. Below is a simulated memorandum. Rewrite it to increase readability.

From: Chief, Improvements Office—Big City Housing Authority
To: Staff
Date: March 23, 1984
Reference is hereby made to the commissioner's speech of March 5 dealing with the necessity of maximizing a solution in relation to the substantive and endlessly durable problems of the inner-city and the inner-city society. In accordance with this reference, I would appreciate the extension of maximally optimal suggestions utilizing our state-of-the art knowledge and expertise, for solving the housing problems of the sorely anguished inner-city community in a cost-effective manner.

2. Join ten friends in a circle and ask five, chosen at random, to leave the room. Take out a complicated diagram or painting (cut from a magazine) and show it briefly to the people who remain. Then remove the diagram. Invite one of the people who left the room to return and have one of those who saw the diagram describe it.

Now, ask each of the four people remaining outside to enter the room, one by one. As each enters, let the last person describe the absent diagram.

   a. Does the description of the diagram remain constant? Does each person add or subtract details? Why?
   b. What implications does this exercise have for communication in public agencies?

3. A group of white people are shown a picture of a white and

black man fighting on a train. The white man is holding a razor. In subsequent interviews, the people who saw the picture describe the white man as unarmed and the black man as holding a razor.

    a. What explains this reaction?

    b. What are the implications for effective communication in public agencies?

4. Which of the following is a good rule for a manager to follow in giving subordinates positive strokes? Why?

    a. Wait until the subordinate's performance meets all of the manager's expectations.

    b. Constantly praise every one of the subordinate's acts.

    c. Concentrate on what's good about a subordinate's performance.

5. Briefly explain how a city fire department can use an EDP system to improve information exchange between headquarters and the firehouses. What role should headquarters, crews, and EDP specialists play in planning and implementing the system?

6. The Project Management Staff (PMS) is a high-level group of advisors attached to the mayor's office in downtown Coldville. Most members of the PMS have MPA degrees from top-grade universities.

Tom Brockton, a PMS member, was told to develop and distribute a seventy-five page plan for the North Coldville Sanitation Program (NCSP), a garbage-collection project funded through a special federal grant. NCSP's office is in North Coldville, a low-income neighborhood, located about half an hour from PMS headquarters.

As soon as Brockton received his assignment, he visited NCSP's office. There, he spoke to Micaela Rivera, the project director, who knew a great deal about the North Coldville community and day-to-day project activities. Brockton thanked Rivera for her time and promised to keep in touch.

During the next two months, Brockton worked steadily on the report, using PMS's well-stocked library to check figures and statements for accuracy. At no time did he contact Rivera, nor did she contact him.

On the due date, Brockton submitted his report. PMS sent a

copy to Rivera who claimed that it contained critical omissions—a claim backed up, to some degree, by Brockton's superiors. Rivera demanded that PMS revise the report, and it was revised at a significant cost in time and effort.

    a. What factors inhibited communication between Tom Brockton and Micaela Rivera?

    b. If you were the head of PMS, how would you prevent a reoccurrence of this situation? Explain how you would structure relations between your staff and the directors of various neighborhood projects.

7. It was 5:40 P.M. on a cold Friday. George McKinnon, head of a federal agency's audit section, was ready to go home when the office phone rang. "Can you come skiing tomorrow?" his friend asked.

"Skiing! With all the work that I have to do! I'll be lucky to get a chance to sleep. Every junior auditor in my unit has written reports this week and I have to go through each and every part with a fine tooth comb. If I don't, how will I know that these babies and their first-line bosses have done the thorough job that I used to do? It's a rough life, I'm telling you. They just don't make workers like they used to."

    a. What is George McKinnon's problem?

    b. How should he solve it?

    c. Assume you are George's friend. Sell your solution to him. Actually explain how you would convince George to change his behavior, being as specific as possible.

UNIT THREE

Effective Oral Communication

9
Communicating Orally:
How and What to Say

Oral communication is critically important to agency life; induction of new administrators, discipline, client contact, staff meetings all depend on the manager's speaking ability. Yet while most administrators are comfortable talking to peers, many are nervous speaking to superiors, subordinates, or even to colleagues from other units.

Fortunately, speech is learned behavior, and training can both reduce anxiety and develop latent talent. This unit offers a practice-oriented guide to communicating orally in agency situations.

VOICE, GESTURES, AND ORGANIZATION

Effective agency communication requires, as a minimum, that administrators use voice and body language clearly and that they structure messages for maximum impact. Let us examine what is meant by clear voice and gesture and by effective organization.

Voice

Six characteristics of a good speaking voice are: adequate quality, pitch, rate, articulation, pronunciation, and variety.[1] We can examine each in turn.

Quality. An effective voice has a pleasing quality based on mellow, full tones and *resonance*, the ability to hold and reinforce sounds. It is free from nasality, hoarseness, and tension.

Pitch. Pitch refers to the habitual tone level a speaker uses as well as inflections and emphases. Too little inflection produces monotony; too much sounds forced. Effective speakers vary inflection to reflect meaning. For example, see how your own pitch varies when you pronounce the word *oh* as a (1) question, (2) statement of anger, (3) expression of lack of concern, or (4) announcement of great enthusiasm.

Rate. Rate refers to the speed of speech and the duration given sounds, words, and phrases. Effective speakers adjust rate to the material and the audience, speaking slowly when their listeners have to weigh statements with care.

Articulation. Effective communicators speak distinctly. Their words are easy to understand without having an exaggerated preciseness that sounds pretentious.

Most articulation problems occur with consonants because vowels (*a, e, i, o,* and *u*) are made with the open mouth. Administrators should be particularly distinct in uttering unvoiced consonants (e.g., *s, t, f, d,* and *g*).

Pronunciation. Today's officials have greater freedom in pronouncing a large vocabulary of words than their counterparts before the 1960s. The stress now is on sounding natural rather than stiff or ostentatious. Furthermore, correct pronunciation can reflect dialects from the region where particular administrators were born.

Dictionary use improves pronunciation. Look up words you come across in print and do not know how to pronounce. Take particular care in pronouncing words that have similar sounds but quite different meanings. For example, pay attention to *accept* and *except, respectively* and *respectfully, statue* and *statute,* and so on.

Variety. Appropriate speech requires variety of rate, pitch, force, and quality. In an effective message, words of great consequence stand out by getting greater force or longer duration.

Evaluating the Six Qualities. If you want to know the state of your own voice, make a tape recording and listen to it. To record effectively:[2]

1. Use a high-fidelity tape recorder or borrow one from a university or other location.

2. Select a five-minute text on a topic related to public administration.

3. Practice reading the text before recording so that you are familiar with it.

4. Test the equipment for proper microphone distance and volume.

5. Begin reading, remaining as relaxed as possible.

Many people do not recognize their own voices the first time they hear them on tape. The disbelief arises because the body's resonance distorts how people hear their own words.

Listen to the tape several times, playing back small parts and paying attention to the sound of individual words. Try to identify imperfections such as strained pitch, mispronunciations, slurred endings, monotonous tones, and a rate that is either overly fast or slow. Do a thorough job of self-evaluation. Only by recognizing flaws can you correct them.

Reading aloud is an excellent way of improving voice quality. Choose several two or three minute selections from a public administration text or an agency report and concentrate on improving your sound. Do you speak too quickly? Pay attention to slowing the tempo. Do you slur endings? Concentrate on forcing your mouth to shape each letter and sound.

After a month of reading aloud, return to the tape recorder. Check your progress; if you noticed flaws on the first tape, you are likely to hear an improved quality on the second.

Gestures

Body language plays an important role in face-to-face communication because each administrator has a unique way of moving his hands and face during conversation. Some gestures push a message across. When a manager praises a subordinate's report, the smile is part of the positive message.

Other gestures hamper communicating. If an administrator runs his finger across his nose, chin, or ear, the audience follows the finger and ignores the message. A manager jingling keys while he gives on-the-job training may cause the new administrator's attention to wander. And if the commissioner constantly looks at her watch during the staff meeting, the gesture contradicts her pleasant opening, "Tell me everything. I have plenty of time."

If you want to evaluate your own use of gesture, videotape a three-minute talk. Prepare a general outline in advance but refrain from using a text or notes during the actual session. Simply talk as naturally as possible before the camera.

Then, play back the videotape several times. Examine your posture, hand gestures, and facial expressions. Do you slouch? Do your eyes wander? Do you sway back and forth? Do you have any nervous ticks? Jot down any mannerisms that detract from the force of your message. Then, practice speaking in front of a full-length mirror for a few minutes each day, watching your use of gestures and consciously suppressing those that irritate.

Structure

Every oral communication has an organizing principle, the overriding factor that determines how sentences are selected and how parts relate to each other. Effective organizing requires that the parts cohere logically, that the audience can move easily from one point to the next, and that the communication contain sufficient information to satisfy listeners.

The best organizing structure depends on the purpose of the speech and on the audience. The six kinds of structures listed below are all useful in different situations.[3]

Chronological order. Main points follow one another in a positive time sequence. This approach is particularly good for explaining agency processes. For example, a manager sends two state reviewers to examine the records of a local agency. The manager explains, "First you call and set up an appointment with the local director. Then hold a conference with him and the unit chiefs." The reviewers follow the directions easily because they know they proceed in a logical, time-oriented sequence.

Spatial organization. Main points are arranged on a geographical framework. This structure is often used in discussing field operations. When an associate commissioner talks to the chief about police corruption, he may start with problems in the most northern precinct and work his way through the various commands. The commissioner follows the discussion easily because he knows where the speaker is headed.

Inductive reasoning. Main points move from the more specific to the more general and so provide a useful structure for reporting programmatic information. For example, a state welfare administrator opens a meeting on eligibility enforcement by saying, "In 1981, the statewide ineligibility error rate was 20.5 percent. In 1982, it is 12.5 percent, and upstate districts have an error rate of 8.3 percent. Yes, we can proudly say that eligibility enforcement is higher today than it was a year ago." The last sentence gathers together the earlier figures and gives them coherence.

Deductive reasoning. Main points move from the general to the more specific. Deductive structure stands induction on its head. The same welfare administrator might use a deductive structure by saying, "We are proud that eligibility enforcement is higher today than it was a year ago. In 1981, the statewide ineligibility error rate was 20.5 percent. In 1982, it is 12.5 percent, and upstate districts have an error rate of 8.3 percent."

Problem-solution. The speaker identifies a problem and then suggests one or more possible solutions. For example, an official in the new federal Department of Education discusses poor student performance on standardized tests with her chief. She identifies the problem and then suggests possible solutions: federally funded reading programs, a national corps of teaching assistants, etc. Problem-solution is a common structure, so it is easy for listeners to follow.

Causal construction. This is a more complete version of problem-solution. The speaker examines the causes of the problem and analyzes anticipated consequences of each solution.

The federal administrator might explain that the student's poor performance is caused by insufficient staff; therefore, the use of teaching assistants frees teachers to work more efficiently. Causal structure can satisfy an audience by giving more information than problem-solution.

Content

Public managers communicate most effectively when they know what information the audience has. Then they calibrate their talk so as not to belabor the obvious or omit facts the listeners need to know.

When an issue is controversial, a question arises whether the manager should include both sides. Some managers fear that presenting arguments that oppose their own point of view raises unnecessary doubts. Other officials counter that fairness requires identifying all opinions.

Research suggests that the decision to include both sides depends on the education and conviction of the audience. Giving both views is more effective with a relatively well-educated (high school graduate or better) audience which already opposes the manager's stand.[4] It gives the presentation an aura of fairness, shows that the manager respects the audience's right to hear all relevant views, and allows the speaker to rebut opposing stands to the degree possible.

Presenting both sides has a negative influence if the audience already agrees with the communicator. This is particularly true if the audience is unaware of the opposing arguments. In this case the communicator plants unnecessary doubts about the success of his or her own policies.

INTEGRATING STYLE AND SUBSTANCE

So far, this chapter has concentrated on identifying skills in voice, gesture, structure, and content. Actually, in the act of speaking, these skills should be automatic. Administrators must know their subject matter thoroughly and be stimulated to convey it to others. Moreover, to be successful at integrating the style and substance of a presentation, the speaker must develop a feeling of mutuality with the audience. He or she must not be afraid of criticism and must have confidence in what is shared with the audience, namely a positive orientation to agency goals. Most important, an effective speaker must understand the particular needs of the listeners and plan the opening and content of the speech accordingly.

Opening

An effective communicator opens presentations in a way that captures attention and ties the subject to audience interests. He may ask a question: "Have you ever stopped to think how much time you spend preparing reports?" She may pique an audience's curiosity: "In the next ten minutes, I'm going to show you how to save an hour a day." Or he may simply announce the relevance of a subject: "Let me tell you how the new EDP system gives you more time to work with clients." Whatever the approach, the speaker opens the presentation with an eye to the audience's point of view.

Content

An effective speaker makes it easy for the audience to follow the presentation. One tactic is to share the structure with the audience. For example, if the structure is problem–solution, the manager begins by noting that she will identify a problem the unit has processing reports and offer several possible solutions. Then, she describes the problem in greater detail and analyzes alternative ways of reducing it.

Another tactic is to tie the talk together by maintaining a consistent attitude. Use the same kind of vocabulary throughout. Plan transitions to link parts: "Remember that we identified . . ." or "Based on that report . . ." A strategic use of summary also aids integration. A skilled communicator repeats ideas that need emphasis, varying the words but not the meaning.

The best oral communications are delivered extemporaneously. Plan talks in advance but never read a speech at meetings or during a training session. Manuscripts restrict body movement, hand gestures, and eye contact. Reading prevents the addition of a phrase that seems appropriate at the moment. (Notes on index cards are all right for long talks, but keep them to the minimum necessary for establishing logical sequence and reminding you of dates, names, and places.)

Try to make presentations two-way affairs. At the very least, welcome questions. (They are the best gauge of how well a communicator puts his message across.) Two-way communication builds rapport, the foundation for effective oral presentation.

10
Training

An agency's performance depends directly on how well it trains employees. Training unifies a diverse set of individuals and transforms them into representatives of a particular organization. It teaches them how to carry out policies, perform specified tasks, and display productive attitudes in both intra- and inter-agency encounters. Proper training also raises morale since, we can assume, competent officials get greater pleasure from their work.

Training is a complex process that we can divide into induction and postinduction phases. Induction includes the new employee's orientation from the personnel department, the agency's handbooks, union contracts, and face-to-face contacts with his immediate superior and colleagues. The postinduction period includes on-the-job training handled by the line manager and offsite workshops sponsored by the personnel department or outside organizations.

We could write a whole textbook on effective communication

during training. The focus in this chapter is much narrower, however, and centers on the manager's role. The goal is to explore appropriate on-the-job techniques managers use to train administrators both during orientation and afterwards.

The chapter is divided into three sections. The first identifies a model of the learning process, analyzing the relationship between learning theory and successful job instruction. The second and third offer tactics for two crucial training situations: orientation and coaching managers.

A MODEL OF LEARNING

Reduced to basic terms, the learning process consists of three phases: input, output, and feedback.[1] Input consists of a manager's instructions to trainees. Output is the trainee's response, the attempt to recall or apply knowledge. In feedback, the manager tries to let the trainees know how well they are doing; the manager explains which responses have been learned and helps the trainees set realistic goals.

Input

During the input phase, the manager first motivates the employee and then explains a process or procedure by reviewing each step thoroughly.

Motivation. For administrators to learn, they must be motivated; few things are as frustrating as trying to absorb material you think is of little or no use.

In New York, for example, state auditors complained when superiors told them *how* to complete worksheets but failed to explain *why* they needed the figures. In California, police had some difficulty learning search procedures—until the trainer told them about officer injuries that resulted from improper search.

Successful trainers create an urge to learn. They build interest by explaining the purpose of each new act.

Explanation. Once motivation is high, managers go through the entire process with the employee(s). They explain in detail each step; where applicable, they amplify oral descriptions with illustrations and demonstrations on agency equipment.

Flowcharts are a particularly effective tool in the training workbag since they depict in chronological sequence all of the essential steps in an agency process. Alternative actions (if available) are identified along with the consequences of each.

Figure 10.1 is a flowchart that shows an administrator in an agency's staff training unit how to respond to line department requests for offsite workshops. It identifies eleven separate steps that the administrator takes if all goes well and alternative procedures in case the request must be denied or consultation between the training director and the line manager is needed. Even a competent manager might have difficulty explaining all the steps verbally. But an employee can follow the sequence without trouble merely by scanning the diagram.

Rules of the game. During explanation, pace is slow, tone pleasant, and diction clear. The manager keeps language simple and free from jargon unless he and the employee share a technical background.

Successful instructors understand that each employee brings a unique background and capacity to the job. They take this into consideration in setting training time and selecting examples and comparisons. For example, let us assume an EDP specialist with extensive military background reports to his new job at a social service agency. If the manager is familiar with defense programming, she can increase training efficacy by comparing the administrator's new responsibilities with his old ones.

Effective trainers keep in mind that few (if any) employees catch all the ramifications of an assignment at first hearing. To increase comprehension, they repeat key statements varying the words slightly.

Managers also try to anticipate questions. They discuss possible problems and solutions that have worked for others in the past. When a process is tricky or difficult, they reinforce oral instruction with a follow-up memorandum.

Checklist. Here is a checklist a manager can use to assess input:

1. Has sufficient time been scheduled relative to the topic?

2. Is the purpose of the new process or procedure well defined?

3. Has the material been developed in a logical, well-organized way?

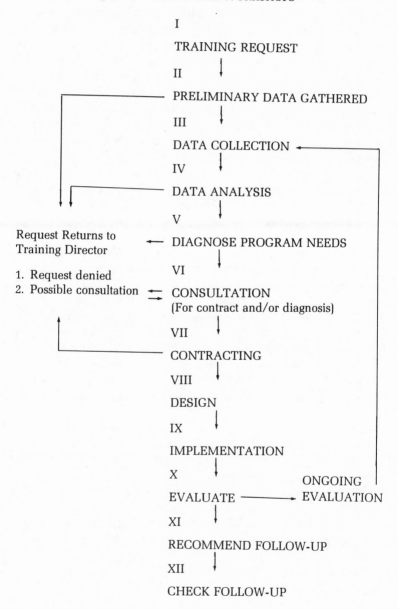

FIG. 10.1. SAMPLE FLOWCHART: RESPONDING TO
REQUESTS FOR OFF-SITE WORKSHOPS

I
TRAINING REQUEST

II
PRELIMINARY DATA GATHERED

III
DATA COLLECTION

IV
DATA ANALYSIS

V
Request Returns to   DIAGNOSE PROGRAM NEEDS
Training Director

1. Request denied   VI
2. Possible consultation   CONSULTATION
                           (For contract and/or diagnosis)

VII
CONTRACTING

VIII
DESIGN

IX
IMPLEMENTATION

X   ONGOING
EVALUATE   EVALUATION

XI
RECOMMEND FOLLOW-UP

XII
CHECK FOLLOW-UP

4. Have you stayed with the stated topic (no excursions into unrelated or irrelevant material)?

5. Have facts, examples, and comparisons relevant to the use of the process or procedure in the particular agency been presented?

6. Have facts, examples, and comparisons relevant to the unique background(s) of the audience been presented?

7. Have you responded adequately to questions and requests for further information?[2]

8. Have you used language appropriate for the particular audience?

9. Have illustrations, flowcharts, and demonstrations where possible been used?

10. Have resources and materials necessary for the process or procedure been documented?

11. Have you analyzed clearly any problems other administrators have come across in relation to the process or procedure and relevant solutions?

12. Have you repeated key statements?

13. Have you dispatched a follow-up memorandum?

Output

Learning theorists stress the importance of thorough practice.[3] Skills that we use grow stronger; those that we neglect fade. Managers err if they do not provide sufficient practice time. It is important that learners try their hand as soon as possible. Immediately after the input phase, the trainee should receive a chance to apply knowledge under close supervision. As mastery grows, administrators need increasing independence.

Let us assume a welfare supervisor tells a caseworker to create a nonthreatening atmosphere with clients. The caseworker agrees that this is a good idea. Supervisor and subordinate discuss various approaches; the caseworker understands the intellectual content of each but is unsure how to proceed. She needs an opportunity to practice with many kinds of clients, an opportunity to try out different paths. It is only by practicing in real life or simulated client-administrator situations that the caseworker can apply the supervisor's instruction and improve her skills.

Feedback

Learners not only need to practice, they must also know how well they are doing. As knowledge of performance increases, learning grows. Ideally, feedback follows immediately on performance. The longer the delay, the less impact it has.

Whenever possible, managers should give feedback before administrators repeat errors; people can *learn* to do a job poorly as well as "right." Too often a new bureau chief stops an administrator from using an overlong or slipshod procedure only to be told, "I've been doing it this way for six months."

Three tactics for effective feedback are identified below.

Be specific.   Feedback should be as specific as possible. Tell an administrator, "Your report is poor," and you have told him nothing. Why is the report poor? Insufficient or irrelevant data? Illogical organization? Awkward sentences? The more specific the criticism, the easier it is for the writer to improve.

Include the positive.   An employee needs to know what to do as well as what not to do. A list of errors is insufficient feedback; the learner lacks a notion of how to improve. At the least, the manager should identify the correct responses and, if possible, demonstrate them in a simulated or real situation.

Encourage and praise.   Learners need encouragement and praise. Successful training requires a mixture of criticism and positive strokes, thereby creating a sense of progress that reinforces motivation.

People tend to abandon a goal if it appears impossible. They perceive overwhelmingly negative feedback as a threat they must "tune out." Administrators must believe that they can master skills if they are to learn; a sense of positive movement helps increase the number of desired responses. We shall see in the next section that praise and encouragement are particularly important during orientation.

ORIENTATION

The purpose of orientation is to introduce new administrators to their jobs and their environment. The way this is handled has an important influence on the newcomer's adjustment, progress and eventual contribution.

Whatever their rank, new administrators tend to be a bit nervous and confused. They need information on:

1. salary and deductions;
2. working hours, holidays, and schedules;
3. benefits and sick leave;
4. agencywide rules and regulations;
5. duties and responsibilities of their position;
6. promotion possibilities;
7. their place in the unit; and
8. their relationship to other units, the agency as a whole, and the public.

Generally the personnel department covers items 1 through 4. The employee's immediate manager explains the substance of the job and introduces the new administrator to his or her colleagues.

Unfortunately, some agency managers undervalue orientation. Their own familiarity with the unit desensitizes them to the newcomer's needs. A manager with this attitude may throw a manual and some forms at the new administrator, tell him to read everything thoroughly and then ask if there are any questions. The manager assumes that there will be none because the procedures look easy to him. (He has only done them six hundred times.)

The employee accepts the material and scans it. He cannot understand section six. He rereads the section, still cannot fathom what the writer means, and wonders if he is an imbecile. (After all, the manager seems to think the material is easy.)

The new administrator is reluctant to ask the unit chief questions because the manager seems so busy. Even when the manager returns to check his progress, the new administrator may be so intimidated by that time that he lets all his questions remain unasked. As a result, it may be weeks before the difficulty surfaces.

Successful orientation requires extensive face-to-face communication designed to relieve the new administrator's very natural anxiety.[4] The manager should:

1. Schedule sufficient time. Face-to-face communication takes time. A manager who realizes the importance of orientation,

reserves an adequate block for going over the material *with* the new employee and allows no nonemergency interruptions.

2. Take the initiative. Welcome the employee heartily. Explain that new personnel are not expected to be familiar with all the unit's procedures or terminology. Give assurances that all budget analysts or caseworkers or investigators ask questions during the orientation period. Explain that this makes the manager's job easier.

3. Minimize social fears. The role of the informal group looms large in most administrators' lives. Early tensions center around social isolation as much as possible inability to master skills. Since a threatening climate retards learning, the manager tries to alleviate this concern by introducing the new administrator to several colleagues and encouraging interaction.

A useful strategy is to ask an experienced employee to serve as a *mentor*, delegating to him or her the responsibility for explaining part of the work routine. This gives the newcomer contact with at least one peer and increases the likelihood of legitimate questions. (It also enriches the mentor's job by giving him or her practice in job instruction.)

A manager who schedules sufficient time, takes the initiative and minimizes social anxieties sets the stage for a worthwhile orientation. In the next section, we will see that some of the same strategies are useful when a top official coaches junior managers.

DEVELOPING MANAGERS

Developing managers is one of the most challenging administrative functions. You cannot train subordinates to manage simply by listing rules or asking them to read a manual. Since management involves getting work done through others,[5] neophytes acquire skill only by contact with other people. They need a chance to learn by doing, to make real-world mistakes and have them corrected. They need a chance to unfreeze old patterns of behavior and adopt new forms.

Coaching, a popular word for training managers, is borrowed from the athletic world. A coach observes the team, analyzes the player's performance, and offers suggestions for improvement. A developer of managers does the same.

Most leadership studies indicate, however, that it is bad supervisory practice to keep close watch on a manager's actions, second guessing at every turn. A better method is to give a new manager room to find a personal style and judge the results. Instruction is more effective when the focus is on achievement.

Management by objectives (MBO) is a coaching system geared towards results.[6] Since it is used in many local and federal agencies, we will examine it in some detail.

Management by Objectives

MBO requires extensive two-way vertical communication, including at least two major interviews between superior and subordinate. The process begins when the superior, say an assistant secretary, gives the junior manager a broad statement of her responsibilities and asks her to formulate specific goals for her unit.

In MBO, goals are concrete, short-term targets, easily translatable into strategies and work assignments. Each contains an area of activity and a performance level. For example, an assistant secretary reminds the manager of a public relations unit that her broad responsibility is to publicize agency programs to a particular clientele. The manager of the public relations unit formulates a goal "to produce and distribute 100,000 copies of a brochure on agency programs by February 1983." The assistant commissioner of a social service agency reminds the manager of a quality control unit that his broad responsibility is to reduce ineligibles on the welfare rolls. The unit manager develops a goal of "a 12 percent decrease in the number of accepted ineligibles by March 1983."

First interview. The first interview gives the superior and subordinate a chance to discuss the goals and reach agreement on their suitability. The superior asks the junior manager to bring a written list of suggested goals, and schedules sufficient time to probe each (with the manager), checking to see if they are:

1. clear, concise, and unambiguous;
2. accurate in terms of the end that the manager actually seeks;
3. consistent with the agency's overall policies;
4. within the manager's competence; and

5. useful for the manager's own professional development, where possible.[7]

After substantial give and take, the supervisor may accept the original list or ask for modifications. Where rapport is good, the junior manager feels free to challenge requests for change, and lively debate can ensue.

Finally, an agreement is reached. The result is a commitment by the subordinate to pursue the goals. The superior agrees to judge performance based on their attainment. (This situation illustrates supervision by results rather than by methodology.)

Second interview. At the end of a prearranged period, superior and subordinate meet again to discuss whether the goal has been reached and what can be done to improve performance. The superior gives positive feedback if the manager has met or exceeded the performance level.

If deficiencies exist, the supervisor lets the junior manager analyze them and suggest improvements on his or her own, stepping in only if the subordinate lacks a suitable plan. The heart of MBO is the junior manager's role in setting objectives. A superior who announces, "You goofed. Here are your new goals," simply misunderstands the whole system.

Let us return to the quality control manager who wants to reduce ineligibles by 12 percent and assume that he only achieves a 6 percent reduction. An effective interview gives him an opportunity to identify the deficiency and suggest a cause, perhaps difficulty in locating deserting parents and seeing if they can support clients. He has the responsibility for proposing a supplementary goal that his unit can translate into new work strategies: Increase location of deserting parents by 8 percent.[8]

The supervisor's main role is to encourage thorough analysis and formulation of goals that are both challenging and realistic. He or she also steps in if the subordinate is unable to suggest a cause or a plausible solution.

The subordinate-dominated communication pattern makes MBO a rewarding experience for senior and junior officials.[9] Since junior managers identify the target, their motivation to pursue it is generally high. If they fail, they tend to be receptive to re-evaluation and accepting suggestions from higher-ups. For senior officials, successful use of MBO requires the same skills as effective delegation. They must learn to trust their subordinates and encourage them to plan and organize their own work.

LEARNING THROUGH EMULATION

Hardly a day goes by that agency officials do not train managers under them. The coaching done through formal systems such as MBO pales beside the amount accomplished by example. The old maxim, "Do what I say, not what I do," rarely works in agencies. Subordinates watch how the unit chief handles functions and act accordingly. They only become confused or cynical if a hard-as-nails, authoritarian manager tells them to lead democratically.

More important than explicit coaching is the atmosphere in which it takes place. When bureau chiefs are effective, subordinates emulate them. They learn public management (including communication tactics) through a process of creative imitation, adapting the chief's style to their own needs and personalities. Secure managers accept both the flattery implicit in emulation and the differences that inevitably emerge between the way they manage and the way their subordinates achieve the same results.

The process of training often leads to interviews or personal sessions between superior and subordinate. The next chapter elaborates on the purpose and conduct of these performance appraisal sessions as well as other interviews.

11
Interviews

An assistant commissioner of a state purchasing department evaluates a division chief. The chief wants to know whether she is getting a promotion. One counselor in a county employment agency accuses another of stealing job leads. Soon the two administrators stop talking to each other and refuse to take each other's telephone calls. A technical writer in the Defense Department says, "The director doesn't appreciate me. The most challenging assignments go to other workers." A teacher claims his transfer violates the union contract. He threatens to file a grievance with the chapter chairperson.

The incidents above have two things in common. First, they represent situations with a potential for harming the agency (or one of its units). Second, they are all incidents that an astute manager tries to solve through one-on-one meetings with the division chief, counselor, technical writer, or school teacher.

The typical agency manager conducts a number of one-on-one meetings with subordinates each year to appraise performance, resolve conflicts, handle grievances and, in general, to help prevent or defuse explosive situations like those listed above. Effective interviews should be an extension of the training/ coaching process; they let administrators know where they stand, develop them for promotion, eliminate intraunit friction, and increase morale. Successful interviews thus benefit both the people immediately involved and the organization.

This chapter analyzes strategies for conducting two types of public agency interviews: those that resolve intraunit conflicts and complaints and those where a manager appraises a subordinate's performance. (Strategies for handling grievances are reserved for chapter 12.)

Resolving Intraunit Conflicts and Complaints

The interest in organizational interviewing stems from a series of experiments conducted in the 1930s at the Western Electric Company's plant in Hawthorne, New Jersey. Accordingly, we open the section with some background on these experiments.

Western Electric's Experiments

The researchers who started the famous Hawthorne experiments wanted to isolate the causes of high morale and productivity.[1] To gather data, they conducted a series of interviews with plant workers, using a *directive* or controlled approach—i.e., the interviewers developed a series of questions and asked them, one after another, of the employees.

The interviewers hoped that the workers would tell them all about life in the plant, particularly the employees' reactions to and feelings about this life. To their surprise, the employees gave superficial answers. Some even wandered away from the topic completely and spoke about matters that interested *them* personally.

The researchers then tried a different tactic. They put away their carefully prepared questionnaires and let the workers direct the conversations. Under the new system, employees broached subjects and interviewers listened.

Gradually, the tone, pace, and content of interviews changed, almost beyond recognition. Superficiality disappeared. Workers disclosed feelings and attitudes of hostility and frustration they had long kept bottled up inside them.

This *nondirective* approach benefited the researchers and the employees alike. The researchers got much of the information they wanted. The workers got long-smoldering complaints off their chests and often received greater insight into their own feelings. The Hawthorne studies convinced many managers, in both the public and private sectors, that nondirective (or employee-centered) interviewing is an effective forum for upward communication when employees have on-the-job conflicts or complaints.

Orientation and Techniques

Nondirective interviewing requires a unique orientation and special techniques. The orientation centers on a desire to find out what interviewees think, to understand the meaning incidents have for them.[2] Thus, the purpose of an interview with the county employment counselor might be to find out her perception of the job-lead stealing question and work out a solution with her. The purpose of an interview with the technical writer might be to explore his frame of reference regarding "appreciation" and the steps manager and writer can take to increase productivity and morale.

This employee-centered orientation dictates the most important technique in the interviewer's workbag—active listening. To most people, the phrase *active listening* seems a contradiction in terms. Listening is generally regarded as a passive activity; you keep quiet and let the other person speak.

To explain what public administrators mean by active listening we can examine some of the activities of managers when they execute a successful interview. Active listeners exercise the following techniques:

1. *Patience and friendliness.* They indicate by verbal and nonverbal signals that they want to listen to the person being interviewed. They smile, sit upright, and do not allow their attention to wander.

2. *Open judgment.* They listen with an open mind, evaluat-

ing the situation after (not before or during) the employee's presentation.

The temptation is sometimes overwhelming to interrupt an administrator and tell him just how wrong he is, particularly if he launches into a personal attack or snipes at colleagues. But such interruptions are always counterproductive; either the employee becomes even more belligerent or the interview comes screeching to a halt.

Active listeners practice restraint. They let the other person make aggressive comments so as to learn more about the employee's position.

3. *A consideration of both manifest and latent content.* Active listeners attend to both what the employee says (manifest content) and what he or she omits (latent content). They are always cognizant that an employee may pass over salient facts and feelings, either because of unawareness or because of deliberate coverup. Active listeners take into account that the interview itself is a social situation between people of different status and so limits uninhibited discussion. Working within these constraints, they decide which latent areas to explore with indirect probes.

4. *The use of probes to keep the conversation going.* Since the interview exists to solve a problem, managers must elicit as much information as possible. To this end, they may have to abandon a nondirective approach temporarily and steer the discussion tactfully.

One technique is to use stock probes such as, "Can you tell me more?" Another is to repeat the employee's own words in the form of a question. For example, if the employee says, "It's impossible to make that deadline. The printer is always late," the manager can probe for more information by asking, "You say the print shop is always late?"

5. *Summarization.* One of the most effective strategies for strengthening dialogue is for managers to summarize an interviewee's position. By summing up the employee's ideas (without judging them), active listeners show that they are paying attention. This recognition alone may spur the employee to say more.

Moreover, because of selective perception, an interviewer often misinterprets nuances of an employee's case. When the manager sums up, the employee has an opportunity to restate his or her ideas and clarify any misunderstandings. The act of summarizing forces the manager and the employee to agree on the nature of the employee's complaint even if they disagree on the appropriate solution.

6. *Respect for the existence of different perceptions of a situation.* Many statements the employee makes can neither be proved true or false. They represent perceptions of a situation that may look very different to other people. Since active listeners understand that different people may perceive a situation in different ways, they can summarize various employees' stories accurately without assuming that any given account is a statement of fact generally accepted by all members of the unit.

7. *Considerations of action.* The purpose of agency interviews is to arrive at a course of action. Ideally, the employee proposes the solution based on his or her own understanding. However, if the employee's solution is counterproductive in terms of agency goals, the manager directs his or her attention to viable alternatives, leaving the employee as much leeway as possible in choosing among them. The aim is to encourage the employee's initiative while at the same time arriving at a solution that is acceptable to both the agency and the individual.

8. *Consultation of outside sources, when appropriate.* Most conflict interviews end when manager and administrator agree on a course of action. But some problems are thorny enough to resist solution in one session. The manager then has to consult outside sources.

A case involving off-the-job difficulties (e.g., alcoholism, drug abuse) requires consulting the personnel department to see what programs the agency sponsors for administrators with these problems. A conflict revolving around several members of a unit requires a series of interviews with the administrators involved. (It almost goes without saying that anything one administrator reports during an interview is confidential and cannot be repeated without permission.)

After the manager consults personnel or other administrators, he or she holds a supplementary interview with the employee from which a course of action emerges.

9. *Maintenance of a behavioral orientation.* At an effective conflict interview, the manager's interest centers on improving the employee's on-the-job behavior. But some agency managers become so engrossed in looking for hidden causes that they overuse psychiatric concepts and techniques in an attempt to explain the administrator's deep-seated motivations.[3]

For example, a social worker tells his supervisor that he cannot meet a reporting deadline because of a particularly heavy client caseload. If the supervisor asks a question like, "Are you repressing your true motive?" this places the interview on another level of inquiry. Such an exchange in the work place increases hostility and inevitably precludes the supervisor's learning about possible deficiencies in scheduling.

Psychiatric techniques can be used with complete safety only in a professional setting where the client's interests dominate the practitioner's actions. In a conflict interview, the agency's interests dictate the manager's actions; an all-out assault on underlying motives is, therefore, both inappropriate and dangerous.

Since behavior within the agency is the manager's concern, he or she wants the administrator to change on-the-job actions in order to increase effective performance. Towards this end, the manager probes for motives only when they have a bearing on observable action and refrains from proposing solutions that require the employee to change personal characteristics. "So, we agree, from now on, you and Linda Smith will share a job file," is an appropriate response to the employment counselor who claims her job leads are being stolen, not "So, we agree, from now on, you will stop being jealous of Linda Smith."

10. *The use of followups.* Some time after the interview, the manager checks implementation of the solution. This involves reviewing whether the employee is following the proposed course of action, and, in serious situations, inviting the employee to discuss his or her progress at a second session. Here, again, the manager follows all of the active listening rules.

Developing Skills

Effective interviewers are made, not born; active listening is a skill we learn by practice. New managers need to experiment until they find the style that works best for them. As they practice, they learn to vary their approach with different people.

A good introductory exercise requires no equipment more complicated than a piece of paper, a pen or pencil, and a casual acquaintance (not a close friend). Ask your acquaintance if you can conduct an interview about a job or school related conflict that he or she wants to resolve. Using the nondirective approach, try to find out his perception of the situation.

Try to follow the rules of active listening; place the interviewee at ease and encourage him to dominate the interaction. Use probes if you need more information.

After the interview, summarize in writing what you have learned. Give the summary to the interviewee and ask him to comment on it, particularly noting any omissions he thinks are important and any misunderstandings.

Then, ask yourself: (1) Why did I omit this point? Did I fail to "hear" it? Did it appear unimportant to me because of my own frame of reference? and (2) Why did I misunderstand the interviewee's perceptions? What can I do to increase my empathy and feelings of mutuality?

You can use feedback from mock interviews to improve your technique until you reach a stage where you automatically elicit relevant detail about a given situation. At that point, when you hand your summary to the person you have interviewed, he or she inevitably says, "That's the problem. That's what's happening. That's exactly what I told you."

Developing skills in eliciting information has payoffs beyond the ability to conduct a successful interview to resolve complaints. Most agencies currently mandate that managers evaluate subordinates periodically and discuss the appraisals with them. The ability to elicit information and avoid misunderstandings is crucial to the success of these interviews as well.

The following section examines three methods for handling

performance appraisal interviews. The argument is that each strategy has its own unique advantages and disadvantages; hence, each is appropriate in different situations.

PERFORMANCE APPRAISAL INTERVIEWS

In his very useful book on the subject, Norman R.F. Maier notes that no universally effective strategy exists for conducting performance appraisal interviews. "Tell and Sell," "Tell and Listen," and "Problem Solving" may each be the "best" approach depending on the particular objectives and personalities of the people involved.[4]

Tell and Sell

The aim of the Tell and Sell interview is to let the employee know where he stands and then get him to follow a plan for improvement. Accordingly, the manager *tells* the employee how he did on the rating and *sells* him on the need for improvement.

An advantage of Tell and Sell is that it is the quickest interview form and frees the manager for other activities. It works relatively well with inexperienced administrators, those who prefer authoritarian leadership, and those who agree with the manager's rating.

Tell and Sell fails when the subordinate disagrees with the manager's assessment. This makes him defensive and bitter, hardly putting him in a state of mind to benefit from the "sales" pitch. The resulting animosity can result in lower performance, particularly in the areas criticized.

Tell and Sell implicitly communicates to the employee that managers know best. Tell and Sell managers may say that they want subordinates to take the initiative but their one-way communication style indicates that they really expect employees to be docile followers. Under Tell and Sell, administrators find it hard to separate doing a good job from getting their supervisor's approval.[5]

Tell and Listen

The aim of the Tell and Listen interview is to communicate the appraisal and let the employee respond. The manager begins the session with a description of the employee's strengths and weaknesses; then, the employee analyzes the rating, indicating whether he or she perceives the manager's assessment as accurate.

As its name implies, Tell and Listen requires active listening skills. Accepting the assumption that his own appraisal contains flaws, the manager encourages the employee to disagree. He uses probes to elicit more information, where necessary. He summarizes the employee's position, pausing to let the junior administrator add corrections and clarifications.

Tell and Listen has two principal advantages. First, it engenders less tension and hostility than Tell and Sell. Employees have an opportunity to present their case; therefore, they can listen to the manager without loss of self-esteem. This makes it far less likely that they will "tune out" useful suggestions.

Second, managers profit from upward communication. While stating his or her case, the employee often makes valuable suggestions about on-the-job responsibilities and expectations. An astute supervisor can learn much about his own failures in training or motivating merely by listening to a subordinate talk. (It takes an exceptional manager to learn from a subordinate; the insecure feel psychologically committed to upholding their own evaluations.)

The chief disadvantage is that some employees may leave the office without knowing precisely where they stand. This makes it difficult for them to follow a specific program of development.

Problem Solving

The aim of the Problem Solving interview is to develop the employee. Hence, communicating the manager's appraisal is not a goal and this strategy makes no provision for directly transmitting performance ratings.

Problem Solving is an employee-centered strategy. Administrators analyze their own performance and suggest improvements. The manager acts as a nondirective interviewer, eliciting subordinate perceptions and helping employees to understand the overall implications of their jobs. Problem Solving works well with MBO because the administrator has a goal against which to measure performance. The two major MBO interviews are Problem Solving sessions.

Two assumptions underlie Problem Solving interviews. First, the manager assumes that he or she and the members of the unit share a mutual goal—they both want performance to improve. Second, the manager assumes that members of the unit can identify their own weaknesses and prescribe correctives. They have both facility at analyzing behavior and familiarity with agency resources for promoting change.

Problem Solving requires a manager with extensive listening skills. The interviewer's repertoire of questions, summaries, and well-timed pauses motivates the employee to think constructively about performance.

There are several advantages to this kind of interview. First of all, Problem Solving stimulates original thinking. It reaffirms that the agency expects administrators to make independent judgments. Problem Solving also reduces negative feelings towards the manager and the interview process, for the junior administrator receives little or no criticism. And it increases the probability that the employee will accept the need for change. After all, the employee identifies the problems and the solutions. Finally, Problem Solving gives the manager an opportunity to learn from subordinates, even though not all managers accept this opportunity.

The weakness of Problem Solving stems from its underlying assumption that all employees can pinpoint their own deficiencies and propose constructive solutions. In actuality, some administrators can, others cannot. Since the agency has to maintain reasonable performance levels, the manager must step in if the subordinate is unable to develop a useful plan. Generally, this means switching from Problem Solving to Tell and Listen.

Also, the Problem Solving format may violate certain union agreements that mandate employees' rights to see a manager's appraisal of their performance. To circumvent this problem, some agency managers schedule two interviews. At the first session, the employee analyzes his or her own strengths and weaknesses and identifies a development plan. At the second meeting, the manager gives an appraisal. This approach encourages employee initiative while ensuring adequate feedback. But the fact of an upcoming appraisal by the manager may inhibit a totally candid analysis by the employee at the first interview.

CONCLUSION

Appraisal is such a sensitive area that no single method always staves off hostility and tension while meeting the goals of manager and subordinate.[6] The onus is on each agency executive to practice a variety of approaches until he finds the repertoire that works best given his unique background, situation, and subordinates.

Interviews are assuming an increasingly important role in agency communication patterns. They offer an opportunity for face-to-face communication and vertical interchange.

The key to conducting most conflict resolution and performance appraisal interviews is a psychological commitment to learning as much as possible about the employee's point of view. The central technique is active listening, the ability to hear what is actually said and meant—not what the interviewer wants to hear.

Moreover, successful interviewers have learners' orientations. They expect to gain from the session. They do not encourage the employee out of a routine sense of duty, but rather out of an understanding that mutual interchange is the best way of achieving their own goals and those of the agency.

12

Grievances

In the last twenty years, unions have become a major ingredient in the public personnel process. The federal government granted its employees the right to bargain collectively in 1962; currently, thirty-five states give their administrators the same privilege.[1] Unions represent approximately sixty percent of the federal work force[2] and over one-third of all nonteaching fulltime employees of states, counties, cities, school districts, and special authorities.[3]

Public sector unions represent blue- and white-collar employees. At the federal level, over half the white-collar workers are represented.[4] In local jurisdictions, even supervisors sometimes have full collective bargaining rights. For example, in New York City, school principals and fire officers have their own unions.[5]

THE FUNCTIONS OF UNIONS

Unions exist to negotiate and administer collective bargaining agreements. An important part of their function is to protect members from unfair treatment and contract violations. In general, public sector contracts negotiated in the sixties had a narrow scope, devoting themselves primarily to salaries and fringe benefits. Today, however, the scope of contracts is much broader. Teacher agreements include provisions on transfers, schedules, class size, student discipline, curriculum, and inservice training.[6] Police contracts tell the department how many officers it can put in a patrol car; social service contracts mandate maximum case loads.[7]

The growth of contract scope has an important effect on public employees, managers, and the policy process. Employees often see the union as an antidote to a faceless and uncaring management. They feel that the contract gives them a say in how they do their jobs. They no longer have to do anything the manager wants but can seek relief through collective bargaining.

Managers often feel the union complicates their job. They have to keep more accurate personnel records to support the agency's position in case of a grievance. They have to take greater care to treat all employees consistently even if they would like to reward star performers with first choice in schedules. The contract restricts managers' latitude in areas where, historically, they had great power.

Yet, by and large, public managers are not antiunion. Often, first-line managers seem to view unions as a golden mean between the "anarchy" of participative decision making and the "outmoded" authoritarianism of unilateral choice. They prefer to collaborate on policy with union representatives rather than with the entire unit (some of whose members may be "unreasonable"); they like the idea that union leaders sell their decisions to the employees. Established unions often want stability as much as managers do and they help to channel discontent and keep it in bounds.

The astute agency manager knows that sometimes his or her aims coincide with those of the union, and sometimes they conflict. After all, an agency is chartered to operate in the public interest. Unions are private organizations created to serve their own memberships. The interests of the public at large and those of a particular group of agency employees can, and often do, differ.

For example, Martin Cullinan, leader of the Levittown, New York, teacher's union, boasts, "The union's first obligation is to its members, not to the students, just as the teacher's first obligation is to his family, not the students."[8] But the agency's first obligation is precisely to the students and not the staff. If the price of union participation is a shunting aside of public goals (as determined by the legislature), then the impact is less democracy in public administration.[9]

Although the concept of public interest is always difficult to define, agency managers have to take public needs and values into account in negotiating and administering contracts. They must judge every interaction according to its influence on the agency's ability to meet legislatively mandated goals.

The principal forum of manager-union interaction is the grievance process, the clearly defined, step-by-step procedures whereby employees initiate and process dissatisfactions stemming from (actual or alleged) contract violations.[10] Handling grievances is an important and sensitive part of the manager's role. (Sometimes unions strike when they think an agency mishandles serious grievances.[11])

The next two sections explore effective techniques for handling grievances. The first section gives an overview of the grievance process itself from initiation to the possibility of arbitration. Following that, we analyze strategies for exchanging information during the initial grievance interview.

THE GRIEVANCE PROCESS

In this section, we follow a simulated grievance in New York City's Human Resources Administration (HRA). Mary Rivera, the grievant, is one type of social service worker represented by the American Federation of State, County, and Municipal Employees, District Council 37. While grievance procedures vary among agencies, all contracts provide for initiation, processing, and resolution stages. Following the simulated case in HRA sheds light on grievance procedures in other organizations.

Initiation

A grievance generally begins when an employee thinks he has been treated unfairly or differently from others. Mary Rivera was angry. She had asked her supervisor for a change in schedule because her brother was sick and she wanted to visit him in the hospital. The supervisor, Don O'Hanlon, refused abruptly. But Mary was certain that he had accepted similar requests in the past. Moreover, her contract specifically stated:

> The Employer, when administratively possible, shall grant an alternate work schedule to an employee who requests such schedule for good and sufficient reason.... Rejection of such request shall be subject to the grievance procedure.[12]

Fortified with this knowledge, Mary visited Anita Gallo, the union representative, and asked her to present a grievance. Anita explained that the first step of the agency's grievance procedure required the employee and/or the union to present the problem verbally or in the form of a memorandum to the designated manager no later than 120 days after the incident occurred.

Anita stressed that most grievances result from oversight or misunderstanding; the majority are solved through verbal interaction at the initiation stage. This is good for the union as well as the agency because problems are settled quickly, in the place they occur and by the people involved, while the facts are still fresh in everybody's mind. Discussion among the administrator, union representative, and manager permits feedback and oral cues, both of which are largely absent from later stages where written channels predominate.[13]

Processing

Despite Anita's optimism, Don fails to grant Mary's request at the initiation interview. He questions whether her reason is "good and sufficient," noting that she can visit her brother during the evenings; he denies that he ever changed a schedule for a similar reason in the past.

Don's rejection only increases Mary's conviction that she is right. Anita explains that it is not always possible to resolve grievances at Step I because honest differences of opinion may exist. The contract provides several appeal stages as a guarantee that the employee is treated fairly even when the immediate supervisor is antagonistic. In Mary's case, the appeal stages include:

Step II An appeal from an unsatisfactory determination at Step I, shall be presented in writing to the agency head or his designated representative who shall not be the same person designated in Step I. . . . The agency head or his designated representative, if any, shall meet with the employee and/or the Union for review of the grievance and shall issue a determination in writing. . . .

Step III An appeal from an unsatisfactory determination at Step II shall be presented by the employee and/or the Union to the Director of Municipal Labor Relations or his designee, in writing. . . . The Director of Municipal Labor Relations . . . shall review all appeals . . . and shall answer such appeals within ten (10) working days.[14]

As union representative, Anita has to decide whether to press Mary's case through the appeals process. Unions screen out problems they consider weak, preferring to concentrate their limited resources on cases where they think they can actually help an employee.

Let us assume that Anita decides to appeal Mary's case. The next step is for the union and manager to translate their oral arguments into writing. Now all the parties have to think carefully about their wording; they cannot change stories midstream. Anita reminds Mary that both management and employee must maintain flexible attitudes. Resolving the grievance may require some give and take on both sides.

Resolution

But suppose Mary loses her case at Steps II and III, when the Director of Municipal Labor Relations concludes that Don acted within managerial prerogative. Does she have any further recourse? Yes, Step IV allows the union to bring a grievance to binding *arbitration*, a process whereby an impartial third party hears the facts and recommends a solution.

Arbitration procedures vary among jurisdictions. Some agencies use a single arbitrator; others use a three-person panel. HRA uses a single arbitrator. Union and agency choose one name from a list of three impartial outsiders prepared by the city's Office of Collective Bargaining.[15]

Anita explains that the arbitrator's responsibility is to give both sides a fair hearing and then make a final decision, or *award*, which is supported in a written review. Unions generally view arbitration as a benefit, a check against managerial inconsistency. Managers are less positive; some feel that only agency officials can appreciate the full consequences of a finding against the department. Both sides realize, however, that binding arbitration affords a neutral way of closing disputes that might otherwise become snarled in the overcrowded court system.[16]

We leave Mary Rivera's grievance in the hands of the arbitrator.

GRIEVANCE MANAGEMENT

Usually an agency wants to solve problems as quickly as possible (unless this means unnecessary capitulation). A grievance resolved at Step I costs less (in time and money) than one going beyond an initiation interview. A grievance adjudicated at Steps II or III is less expensive and wearying than one brought to arbitration.

The employee's immediate supervisor is the key figure in determining how efficiently grievances are handled. The supervisor's communication skills influence the number of grievances in a unit and employee satisfaction with the initiation stage.

In handling grievances, managers want to communicate with employees and union representatives while never losing sight of the agency's mission. They need to encourage employees to discuss their problems fully, taking their suggestions into account when they mesh with the organization's goals.

Specifically, successful grievance handling requires that the manager:

1. Understand the union contract. Managers ought to be thoroughly familiar with contracts covering employees in their

unit. They should read the agreements and discuss them with their own superiors or in special training sessions.

2. Know agency practice. A knowledge of past practice often clarifies the contract. Agreements are written descriptions of terms arrived at during intense negotiations; words that seem clear at the bargaining table may appear ambiguous later.[17] If a problem of interpretation arises, the manager asks, "How did the agency handle this issue in the past?"

Practice, however, cannot offset the clear implications of contract language. As arbitrator Paul Prasow notes, "If the language points in one direction and the practice in another, go with the language."[18]

3. Use active listening. Interview skills can occasion a clear picture of the employee's problem: listen without interrupting or arguing; show interest and concern; use probes to elicit important information including the specific action the employee wants you to take; summarize, repeating the grievance in your own words and encouraging the employee to correct any misinterpretations. Aim for mutual agreement on the facts—even if you cannot agree that a contract violation occurred.

However, not everything the employee says has to be taken at face value. Seek out all the people involved in the incident and encourage them to discuss the dispute together.

4. Know time limits. Be familiar with the time limits for acting on a grievance. As a general rule, the employee should know the manager will investigate the case and make a decision within the time the contract allows. (A few problems can be solved on the spur of the moment but most require focussed analysis; rash decisions can cause untold headaches for the grievant and the agency.)

5. Be flexible. An emphasis on solving the problem rather than on defending a particular act fosters negotiation. When you make a mistake, admit it as soon as possible. Sending the dispute through channels only compounds matters.

6. Confirm the decision in writing. After the manager reaches a decision, the employee should receive a brief memorandum recording the pertinent facts (the contract provision that was allegedly violated, the date, etc.).

If the manager decides that the employee is wrong, he or she should let the employee save face as much as possible. Remember that the thrust of grievance management is to reduce dissatisfaction, not to affix blame. An astute manager words decisions with an eye towards re-establishing harmony in the unit.

7. Learn from the grievance. When an employee presents a grievance, he sends a message to management. The official who processes it has an opportunity to learn whether weaknesses exist in agency practices and, where possible, to make the necessary corrections. A manager should evaluate a grievance broadly, asking himself, "What can I learn from this problem? Are there constructive implications regarding the way we do things in this unit?" Grievances allow managers to gain useful information on employee dissatisfaction, information that can be used to prevent certain grievances from reoccurring.

CONCLUSIONS

Grievance management is a recognized facet of modern agency life. Contracts generally provide for a multiphase step-by-step approach including initiation, processing, and resolution stages. The manager's communication skills influence how many grievances are solved efficiently at the initiation interview, thus saving the agency time and money, and how many escalate into multiphase affairs.

To handle grievances, managers need interview skills, including active listening. They have to encourage employees to discuss problems fully with them and treat those who do so fairly and without rancor. Skills that produce effective day-to-day harmony also contribute to successful grievance management.

13

Staff Meetings

Some observers consider poorly run staff meetings the single biggest waste of time in the public service. The *blocker* disagrees with everyone else at the meeting, particularly on topics all the others want to resolve. The *recognition-seeker* uses the meeting to boost her own ego. The *special-interest pleader* takes others' time to plead his own case. The *withdrawers* converse privately on matters of their own. The *playboy* shows off and tells outrageous stories.[1]

How can the manager avoid this? How can he or she use the meeting as an effective forum for vertical and horizontal communication and a setting for the attainment of agency goals? Successful meetings are hardly a matter of luck. They depend on the manager's ability to lead, a competence built ultimately on careful planning, organizing, and evaluation.

This chapter analyzes strategies for holding effective conferences to seek information, expertise, and judgment from staff; to facilitate teamwork; to set group goals; to locate, analyze, and solve problems; and to give employees an opportunity for interaction. The focus is on the use of meetings to develop interest and motivation, increase participation, and take concrete action towards agency goals.

PLANNING

An effective plan for a staff meeting includes the following requirements:

1. Have an overall conference strategy. Decide the type of issues you will handle through meetings and how often you will call them. Public managers have at their disposal many channels for communicating with staff. They have to decide which information to communicate through meetings and which to interchange through memoranda and personal interviews.

In general, conferences are appropriate when the information is non-routine. Memoranda are the preferred channel for transmitting relatively simple, uncontroversial facts. (Call a meeting if the unit must eliminate two telephones and you want advice on which shall go. Send memoranda to indicate that the switchboard numbers have been changed.)

The appropriate interval between conferences depends on the participants' responsibilities and geographical dispersion. A team of detectives may confer on a difficult case every morning and every night. A group of regional commissioners may fly to Washington, D.C., once a month (or once a year). However, the more frequently conferences are used, the more they contribute to developing an administrative team.

2. Know the objectives of each meeting. Decide the purpose in advance, making the goal as specific as possible. Plan your strategy in terms of achieving the goal.

3. Select participants.[2] Try to keep the group as small as possible; only invite those who can contribute or benefit. Two-way communication is hard to come by when there are more than twenty participants. The audience tends to sit and listen.

Occasionally, special reasons exist for enlarging the circle of invitees. You may ask a junior administrator to a senior staff meeting as a sign of recognition or to boost morale. You might ask principal rivals or antagonists from outside the unit if the purpose is to solve an interunit problem. Experts from other departments may be invited to give indepth presentations. But, in general, keep the roster small.

4. Analyze the group. Try to determine the participants' attitudes and goals in relation to the discussion topic(s). Ask yourself:

    a. What experience does each participant have in this area?

    b. What can each contribute?

    c. What biases and prejudices has each formed?

    d. Is there division in the group; will the topic be controversial?

    e. How can I keep in bounds any conflict that may occur?

Participant analysis provides the key to successful leading; the manager gears the meeting's format to the needs and background of the group.

5. Prepare an agenda. Develop a one-page agenda well in advance of the session. A good agenda gives direction; its lack encourages aimlessness and rehashing of old debates.

The early staff meetings of New York City's Mayor Ed Koch came in for a lot of criticism because no one prepared an agenda. One deputy mayor labeled the meetings "ridiculous" and "disorganized"; another participant noted that without an agenda, events controlled all debate.[3]

A good agenda also gives participants enough information to encourage informed attendance. The heading contains a one-sentence statement of the purpose, date, and place of the meeting as well as the starting and stopping time. (Participants should know in advance how many hours the meeting requires.) The body of the agenda is an outline. The developer lists topics in the order they will be covered. He puts an appropriate notation next to a topic if he wants members to bring written materials (e.g., union contracts, manuals) or if he wants to give out assignments. (Without an agenda, Koch sometimes gave the same assignment to two aides.[4]) The agenda is a tool for organizing communication at the session.

6. Develop an outline. The outline is a guide for the leader, an elaboration of the agenda. The outline consists of a definition of

topics, cues for introductory remarks, and notes for discussion. It includes an approximate timetable for covering each subtopic (if there is more than one); probes and questions for moving discussion along; and a list of audiovisual aids.

7. Select facilities. Administrators are more likely to enjoy meetings held in pleasant, well-lighted rooms. The manager or an assistant makes certain that such a room is available at the specified time, with appropriate facilities (tables, chairs, pads, pencils) and the requested audiovisual equipment. If possible, the room should not have a telephone. A secretary can take calls and receive visitors for people in conference.

A round table is the best seating arrangement for small meetings, because the circular format stresses the equality of all participants and encourages two-way communication. Unfortunately, few tables can accommodate large groups (about twenty or more). Participants are forced to sit in rows facing the leader, an arrangement that reinforces their sense of being in a classroom where "teacher" talks and good boys and girls listen. This lack of adequate facilities is yet another reason for keeping meetings small!

8. Designate a recorder. Ask a participant to take minutes before the meeting. A group secretary ensures a record of decisions while freeing other members to concentrate fully. (It is almost impossible to take copious notes and participate simultaneously.) You may designate one recorder for all sessions or rotate the assignment, depending on group preference.

DIRECTING

Good planning leads naturally to effective on-the-spot direction. At the meeting, the leader should:

1. Start on time. Set a starting time and stick to it. Waiting for latecomers only rewards negligence.

2. Distribute handouts. Handouts serve as useful visual aids and increase attention. Pass out most written material before the meeting, making certain that you have sufficient copies to go around. A particularly helpful item is an agenda with a few blank spaces for participant note taking. This helps people follow the flow of ideas.

3. Follow the agenda. In general, use the agenda to hold the meeting on course, moving from topic to topic in orderly fashion and permitting few side discussions. Occasionally it helps to put the agenda aside for a few minutes and encourage enthusiastic participation, but, as a rule, stick to the outline and the prearranged time allocated for each topic.

4. Set a supportive climate. Conference participants are often afraid to interact honestly with each other. A situation develops where the participants are generally encouraged to express their problems but hesitate anyway:

> Every guy is covering up and is not about to air his own dirty linen. . . . Nor is he going to point the finger at another . . . because they might come right back at him![5]

To avoid this, the leader has to give participants the confidence to talk openly by drawing them out and urging them to elaborate on their analyses. Questions, used as supportive probes, are phrased to elicit more than a "yes" or "no" answer. Positive strokes are offered generously. Astute leaders praise useful contributions, particularly when an administrator criticizes his own performance.

5. Use role playing to defuse tension. Even when administrators are reluctant to discuss their own human-relations problems, they may be willing to take roles in simulated case studies that relate to them. The leader can then use the simulations as a springboard for discussion.

6. Vary leadership style. Appropriate leading varies with the session's goal. If the purpose is to transmit information, control can be kept relatively firm. The leader includes a good deal of one-way communication (to ensure that participants get the necessary facts) and then allocates time for participants to ask questions and offer constructive criticisms. But decision-making sessions need a more permissive climate. The leader wants to encourage spontaneous and enthusiastic give and take. Any display of authority dampens animation; participants are bound to say, "Well the chief thinks this way. Why should I stick my neck out and suggest another plan?"

Osborn suggests *brainstorming* as a good technique for

encouraging creativity in decision-making sessions.[6] The leader identifies a problem and asks members to call out solutions spontaneously. A secretary records all ideas without criticism or screening, the rationale being that a long list is more likely to contain at least some "winners." Only when the entire group runs dry do participants become judge and jury, weeding out undesirable suggestions and combining and improving the others.

Buzz sessions are a second technique for encouraging active participation. The leader breaks the session into small groups to discuss the problem. Discussion is generally intense because each buzz session only contains three or four people who can socialize easily around a small table. At the close of deliberations, each group selects one person to present its findings to the entire meeting.

7. Use appropriate language. An effective leader uses language that everyone at the session understands. The approach varies with the audience. Legal terminology is fine for a meeting of the agency's legal unit. It is inappropriate for a conference on poverty involving lawyers, social workers, and urban housing specialists.

8. Keep on target. Sometimes individual participants try to steer the meeting off course for their own ends. A group discussing performance appraisal may be interrupted several times by Charlie Jones who wants to rehash why he failed to get promoted six years previously.

As much as possible, a good leader lets the group handle such digressions. Peer disapproval is often a more potent weapon than an edict from authority, and enthusiastic groups resent irrelevant sidetracking as much as the leader does.

If peer pressure is unsuccessful in deterring interruption, then try to steer the discussion back to the topic: "I'm glad you mention that, Charlie. It reminds us how important a good performance appraisal system really is." If that fails, appeal to time limits: "That's an important story. But not now! Let's keep the meeting going!" Occasionally it is necessary to speak privately to an administrator who seems to always have his own agenda. If Charlie veers from the path in January, February, and March, tell him, "The April meeting is going to be a tight session. I'd like everyone to stay on course."

9. Summarize. At the end of each topic, list the points that participants agree on. Close the entire session by summarizing decisions made and actions taken; identify issues that the group has resolved and those that will be reopened at a subsequent session. Recapitulation serves as a positive stroke, indicating that the unit is making progress and that meetings have a worthwhile function in agency life.

10. Close on time. Meetings that run over the designated hour wreak havoc with participants' schedules. If sessions habitually bog down, ask yourself two questions: Am I scheduling too many topics? Do I stop side discussions when they start? The first problem requires reappraisal of the overall conference strategy, with the leader either handling some topics through interviews and memoranda or, alternatively, scheduling a greater number of staff sessions. The second problem requires firmer leading and the resolve to talk to certain participants in advance. At any rate, dragging meetings past their allotted hour only makes people restive and less willing to exchange ideas.

Following Through

A staff conference is not an event isolated in time and space from other agency activities. The leader's responsibilities include making certain that decisions are implemented and learning from past mistakes so as not to repeat them. An astute manager evaluates meetings with an eye towards improving future sessions and the unit's day-by-day productivity and morale.

Specific action steps include:

1. Send the minutes. Each participant should receive a résumé identifying date and time of the meeting, who attended, major topics analyzed, and decisions made. Minutes remind participants of what occurred; they show that the leader takes conferences seriously and expects participants to do the same.[7]

2. Evaluate your performance as a leader. Analyze your performance, attempting to maintain a high level of honesty and objectivity. Ask yourself:

- Was the meeting effective?

- Did the group reach its goal(s)?
- Did we have sufficient time to cover all topics on the agenda?
- Was participation enthusiastic?
- Did people speak freely?
- Were there any difficulties keeping the meeting on target?
- Was it difficult to get a consensus on appropriate action to take?
- How were the facilities? Should the group continue to use them?

Use the answers to improve future sessions.

3. Solicit feedback. Rather than relying only on self-evaluation, ask participants for their reactions as well. Some managers do this very informally, simply speaking to two or three people after the session. Others set up *listening teams*. They approach several participants before the conference and ask them to meet afterwards in order to evaluate the session. The listening team then submits its report orally at a mini-evaluation meeting with the manager.[8]

4. Check on action. Check that decisions made at the meeting are actually incorporated into operating procedure. Decide if particular topics ought to be reopened at the next session. At all times remember: a meeting is only effective if it influences day-by-day unit functioning.

Audiovisual Aids

Many managers use audiovisuals to increase attention and clarify ideas at meetings.[9] Almost all the rules that apply to preparing oral presentations apply to developing aids as well, although in the latter case, cost limits are a more significant factor.

Once again, purpose determines presentation (form follows function). The manager first determines why he or she wants to develop an aid and then asks, "Which aid best accomplishes my particular purpose?" Goal first, then strategy. The following subsections identify five audiovisual aids commonly used at agency meetings.

Flipcharts

The flipchart (a standard sized easel and paper) has two functions. During a meeting, the leader can use it to draw outlines and diagrams that have been worked out in advance. Alternatively, it can be used to list participant suggestions, stimulating people to offer more items and to remember those that have been offered. In both cases, the leader writes or prints legibly and largely enough for all to see. Notations are simple and clear, using telegraphic style with unnecessary words and figures eliminated. Since excessive writing disturbs eye contact, the leader often turns around and looks directly at participants.

Slides and Transparencies

Both slides and transparencies are excellent devices for presenting background material to relatively large audiences, although they are generally too expensive for small-group sessions. Slides are made by placing charts, graphs, or brief verbal explanations on plain white paper and photographing them with 35 mm film. Transparencies are produced by drawing or writing on acetate sheets (which are available in art supply stores) and placing them directly in an overhead projector for viewing on a screen.

Simplicity is the key to producing slides and transparencies. Keep words to a minimum because each frame flashes on the screen for only a few seconds.

In a large session, make certain that illustrations can be seen from the back row. Generally, if you can read a two-by-two-inch slide without a magnifier, people in the rear will be able to read it on the screen.[10]

Videotapes

All taping requires reliable equipment and a leader (or assistant) who can run it. (A manager who plans to tape should check first with the agency's media department or specialist to see what they have to offer.)

Relatively large informational sessions make use of two kinds of videotapes: pretaped demonstrations of new techniques and spontaneous role playing where participants at meetings act out simulated human relations problems.

Pretaping. In addition to properly functioning equipment, pretaping demands well-rehearsed, competent "actors" who are familiar with the procedures they demonstrate. Generally, senior administrators or staff people make the best actors because they have skills the manager wants people to learn. For example, a social service manager might show how an experienced caseworker deals with a frightened client in a simulated interview. He might ask an EDP specialist to explain on tape why we fill out computerized forms in a prescribed way. In either case, the manager hopes that the group benefits from the actor's expertise.

Spontaneous role playing.   The purpose of spontaneous role playing is somewhat trickier. The manager wants people to learn from their own behavior. For this, a supportive climate must exist so that people are willing to view their mistakes and profit from them. A manager never offers to tape spontaneous role playing unless rapport is high, communication open, and participation enthusiastic.

Films

Many agencies have (or can obtain) professionally produced management films for background use at large informational sessions.[11] Novice managers seek them out because they have a sophisticated, advertising agency style that inhouse materials lack.

Too often, these films merely serve as decorative filler. Produced for nationwide consumption, they tend to be standardized analyses of concepts such as time management or delegation. They make no attempt to present any of the nuances of a given agency's situation. They cannot duplicate the intricate human relations patterns found in a particular unit.

Occasionally, a professional film is so well constructed and entertaining that it makes a dandy icebreaker or introduction. In general, however, self-made materials have the dual advantage of being unit-specific and much less expensive.

CONCLUSIONS

In the end, the key to successful audiovisuals is the same one that unlocks the door to all effective oral communicating: Let purpose and audience determine content and style. Indeed, as we shall see in the next unit, purpose and audience are essential to written as well as oral exchange. They determine style and content of reports and memoranda as surely as that of face-to-face training, interviews, and staff sessions. Both in speaking and writing, goal determines strategy.

Summing Up
Concepts for Review;
Problems and Exercises

Voice
  quality
  pitch
  rate
  articulation
  pronunciation
  variety
Gesture
Structure
  chronological
  geographical
  inductive
  deductive
  problem-solution
  causal

Training
  input
  output
  feedback
Orientation
MBO
Interviews
  directive
  nondirective
Active listening
Performance appraisal
  "Tell and Sell"
  "Tell and Listen"
  "Problem Solving"
Collective bargaining
Grievance
Arbitration
Role playing
Brainstorming
Buzz sessions
Listening teams
Form follows function

PROBLEMS AND EXERCISES

1. Assume you are a unit chief in a public agency assigned to explain a practice or process to a new administrator. Prepare and deliver a five-minute explanation, asking a friend to role play the new employee. Use flowcharts, equipment, and other props as necessary.
  a. Evaluate your performance as a trainer using the checklist in chapter 10.
  b. Have a group of your peers rate your style and content with the same checklist.
2. Select any public agency in your neighborhood.
  a. Identify and describe its channels for counseling administrators who have on-the-job conflicts or complaints.
  b. Identify and describe its performance appraisal system.

    c. What channels do managers use to communicate appraisals?

    d. Get a copy of a union contract covering one set of administrators and analyze the grievance procedure. Which complaints are covered by the procedure? What are the steps in the grievance process? What provisions are made for arbitration? What limits, if any, are set on the range of issues open to arbitration?

    e. Discuss the grievance process with representatives of agency management and the union. Are each of these administrators satisfied with the present grievance process? What suggestions, if any, do they have for improving it?

    f. Assume you are to set up an "ideal" grievance process for the unit. What would it include? Outline the actual steps, including rules for handling information exchange effectively during each one.

3. Is each statement below an example of good interviewing practice? Defend your answer.

    a. Break in immediately if you disagree with what the employee is saying. He is entitled to hear your point of view.

    b. Serve as a mirror for the employee. Restate his statements, briefly but accurately.

    c. Be polite when you interrupt the interview to take telephone calls and messages.

    d. If you disagree with the employee, let him know it. If he won't accept your point of view, argue!

    e. When the employee is emotionally involved in a situation, get emotionally involved yourself in order to offer genuine support.

4. What is the relationship between MBO and performance appraisal? What type of interview communication pattern would you set up in an agency that uses MBO (Tell and Sell, Tell and Listen, Problem Solving)?

5. Read the following case study and list all the mistakes John Dahl made. Suggest alternative strategies to ensure effective communication at the next meeting.

John Dahl called a meeting of the entire Administration on Aging unit to discuss the time a few members of the field staff were leaving work. (Twice supervisors had discovered entry-level caseworkers finishing their rounds at four-thirty rather than five.)

As thirty people entered a small room, many wondered what topic they would discuss that day. "Are there enough chairs?" Brenda Farley, a field representative, asked. "I guess I'll bring the one in my office."

"Don't worry," her friend laughed. "John will wait for you."

John Dahl began the meeting by observing that everybody in the unit was paid to work from nine to five. He then paused while his secretary came in to deliver a message. While John talked to the secretary, Dan Carlisle, one of the field staff members, raised a question about safety on the streets—one of his favorite topics.

Soon people at the meeting were discussing crime rates and the question of working hours was quite forgotten. John could not decide how to get the meeting back on schedule. He knew that two men had recently robbed Dan on his way to work and John was afraid to appear insensitive. "This meeting is going to take more time than I thought," John said to himself. "Well, I know one way to save time. I won't bother to summarize our conclusions. Everyone's here. They'll get the gist of things."

6. The contract says, "Employees who fail to work the day before or day after legal holidays will not be paid."

    a. As unit manager, do you have any problems interpreting this clause?

    b. If so, how will you resolve them?

UNIT FOUR

Effective Written Communication

14
Collecting and Organizing Information

The importance of face-to-face communication must not obscure the significant role written documents play in agency life. Reports and memoranda are a basic channel of vertical communication. They are crucial to planning, evaluation, and control because they act as a permanent record, offering evidence as to how the agency performs its legislatively mandated tasks.

Two generalizations characterize all effective written communications. First, form follows function; each written document serves some purpose, helping administrators to either reach a decision or undertake acts. Second, memoranda, reports, etc., are not merely "written" at one fell swoop. Preparing written communications is a complex job that requires careful gathering of information and organization. Moreover, good written communications require rewriting and editing so as to assure readability.

A written report stands or falls on its information and structure.

Accordingly, this chapter offers generic advice on collecting and organizing information. Strategies for turning the information into memoranda, summaries, option papers, position papers, progress reports, and training manuals appear in chapter 15.

COLLECTING INFORMATION: SCOPE

The first step in collecting information is to know what you need. It is as much a mistake to present too much data as too little; few agency managers have time to linger over padded reports "impatiently attempting to glean the information they need from ten pages of rubbish."[1]

Appropriate data scope depends on the report's objective(s), audience, length, and due date. Once again, form follows function; information should move a report towards its goal(s). For example, intensive statistical analysis is appropriate in a paper whose objective is to analyze the feasibility of constructing mass transit facilities; it is inappropriate in a memorandum whose purpose is to announce that construction has started. Audience background and needs determine the depth and specificity of the material. A report's length suggests how much research has to be done. A one-page memorandum requires less background analysis than a twenty-page paper. Also, a long deadline means that the writer is expected to consult outside sources. Alternatively, when a manager hands out an assignment saying, "This is due in two days," an overview is appropriate.

It is imperative that an administrator understand goal, audience, length, and deadline as soon as an assignment is received. If there are any questions, he or she should ask the supervisor for immediate clarification.

COLLECTING INFORMATION: SOURCES

The next step in collecting information is to identify appropriate sources for obtaining what you need. Effective communicators are familiar with a variety of sources and choose the best for each presentation. Among the sources that are available to administrators are personal observation, interviews, questionnaires, and published (or secondary) works.

Observation

Personal observation is a quick, economical way of gathering facts. A unit chief observes that employees arrive late; she dictates a note to end the practice. A recreation leader sees a good use of space at another center; he informs his own staff of his discovery.

Personal observation alone rarely gives a solid picture of program implementation or agency activities. First, by definition, the scope is limited to what one administrator sees. Since many agency activities occur simultaneously, the writer who relies exclusively on personal observation cannot possibly get a complete story. Second, personal observation shows how a particular event appears to one observer—but the same event may look very different to other participants.

In summary, personal observation is an adequate basis for a short memorandum. But the writer of progress reports and options or position papers should supplement it with information gained from other sources.

Interviews

As a way of learning how situations appear to other people, interviewing is an effective technique when a report requires knowledge of employees' views on policy or work routines. For example, let us assume an administrator receives an assignment to develop a paperwork simplification program. In order to write the report he has to know which programs are effective and capable of winning the support of employees. After the administrator collects all the forms used by the agency, he interviews a sample of employees on how they process specimens. The interviews give the administrator more information on paperwork than could possibly be gleaned from personal observation along with knowledge on which reforms have the employees' support.

Research interviews require some of the tactics described for oral communications in chapter 11. Again, the interviewer has a specific objective and focusses conversation to receive the information needed. Successful interviewers allot sufficient time for the interview, let the people being interviewed do most of the talking, phrasing questions in language that they understand, and practice active listening using probes as necessary.

Occasionally, an administrator conducts an interview through letters or telephone calls. This is a difficult communication situation because the interviewer cannot establish rapport as easily as in face-to-face exchange. The person being "interviewed" may well feel that the request intrudes on valuable time and ignore it.

To discourage selective exposure, keep written or phoned requests for information as short, clear, and specific as possible. As in all interview situations, include a brief statement on why you need the information and how the eventual report will help the people who provide data.

Questionnaires

Questionnaires are a more formal means of obtaining first-hand information. For projects with relatively long deadlines and ample budgets, they are a useful means of collecting: information from branch and regional offices; data on specific problems administrators encounter; the reasons why administrators make particular decisions; and information on attitudes—what administrators think about their institutions and programs.[2]

As written documents, questionnaires tap a larger population than oral interviews but rarely probe as deeply. They also exact considerable operational costs—the time, money, and staff needed to conduct an adequate survey. Administering questionnaires requires expertise in a whole array of research techniques: designing questions, obtaining a sample of respondents, and coding and analyzing large numbers of responses. In particular, staff must ensure that the questions are worded in a way that elicits data on the topic desired. Poorly written questions either lead to low return rates (administrators simply chuck the survey into the nearest basket) or irrelevant answers.

To avoid these problems, the administrator should:

1. Determine the purpose of the questionnaire. Make certain

that you understand the type of information you are collecting before developing any items.

2. Use questions that are easy to understand. Write questions that are as short and clear as possible. Avoid difficult words and esoteric phrases. Consult administrators outside your specialty if you are afraid that argot or jargon is creeping into any of the items.

3. Design items that respondents can answer. Ask questions that respondents have enough information to answer. Just because you are familiar with a given statute or policy, do not assume that everyone else is also. It makes little sense to ask people if they support revision of Section 2030 unless you are certain that they know the contents of the section.

4. Use objective wording. Try to word questions as objectively as possible, paying particular attention to the connotations of different phrases. Avoid loaded questions that suggest you want the respondent to pick a given answer. Use, "Do you favor participative management?" rather than, "Is participative management harmful to agency structure?"

In sensitive areas, let the respondent know that no "right" answer exists. Begin an item by noting, "In interviews, some people said they were in favor of this policy, some said they were against it. How do you feel?"[3]

5. Set up predetermined categories. Effective questionnaires rarely require much free-form writing on the part of respondents. The developer sets up predetermined categories and asks respondents to check or circle the answer they favor. Frequently used categories include:

1	2	3	4	5
strongly agree			strongly	disagree

1	2	3	4	5
most important			least	important

Predetermined categories make the questionnaires easy to complete. Their use tends to increase the percentage of respondents who return the survey, ensuring more representative, and hence more accurate, information.

6. Arrange the items in logical order. Sequencing drastically affects readability and validity.[4] Use subheadings to distinguish the beginning and end of various topics.

7. Select an accurate sample. Make certain you send the questionnaire to those people who have access to the information you want. If your assignment is to sample the attitudes of principals, it makes little sense to send the questionnaire to school teachers; if the assignment is to identify processes used in regional offices, you cannot limit your sample to headquarters staff.

8. Select a large enough sample for your purposes. Select a sample large enough to meet your predetermined standards for acceptable levels of error.[5] (Appropriate size varies with the statistical tests you use to analyze the data; if you have to select a sample, consult someone who has expertise in statistics and can offer advice geared to your particular requirements.)

9. Pre-test the instrument. Try the questionnaire on a small group of people before giving it a major run-through, making certain that the pretest cohort contains the same type of administrators (in terms of age, sex, race, position, geographical location, etc.) as the major sample.

10. Revise after pre-testing. Revise the questionnaire based on feedback from the small group. Tighten, clarify, and make more concise and brief where possible.

Published Works

A vast array of published material exists on almost every conceivable agency topic, much of it useful as background material in agency reports. Effective use of libraries is an indispensable ability for anyone whose agency responsibilities include much writing. Administrators should have a good idea of the materials contained in their agency's library and the sources available at nearby public and university collections.

The subsections below identify some sources that are often consulted for extensive reports, including encyclopedias, year books, directories, bibliographies, catalogs, indexes, and professional books and periodicals. The appropriate sources to examine in any given case depend, of course, on the informational requirements of individual writing assignments.

Encyclopedias. Encyclopedias are useful as an introduction to a subject with which an administrator is basically unfamiliar. General encyclopedias (of which the best known are the *Encyclopaedia Britannica* and the *Americana*) cover a wide range of subjects at a fairly basic level. Special encyclopedias delve more deeply into one specific field. For example, the *Encyclopedia of the Social Sciences* contains research overviews in sociology, psychology, economics, history, political science, education, and statistics.

Yearbooks. Yearbooks provide statistical data on government operations and political, economic, and demographic trends. For extensive compilations of nationwide data, see the Census Bureau's *Statistical Abstract of the United States, City and County Data Book* and supplementary monthly and quarterly reports. In addition, many federal, state, and big-city agencies publish statistical yearbooks on their own performance.

Directories. Directories are alphabetical lists of people and organizations you can contact for further information on a given topic. Most state and city governments publish directories listing the titles, addresses, and telephone numbers of senior officials. Private firms (such as Bowker) publish directories of professional, labor, and ethnic organizations.

Bibliographies. Bibliographies are alphabetical lists of published works. The most famous is probably *Books in Print* which lists by author, title, and subject all the books that are currently available for purchase in America.

Bibliographies on specific topics are also available. For example, the National Institute of Mental Health publishes annotated bibliographies on ethnicity, race, urban politics, and other sociological topics. Publishing firms offer bibliographies in such relatively esoteric fields as public ombudsmen and other complaint handling systems, police training, neighborhood commercial revitalization, and the role of environmental variables in public decisions.[6] If you want to find out if a bibliography has been written on a given topic, consult the *Bibliographic Index*, a bibliography of bibliographies.

Catalogs. Catalogs are bibliographies prepared by the organization that sells the material. Federal reports (available for purchase) are catalogued in the *United States Public Documents Monthly* and the semi-monthly *List of Selected United States Government Publications.* State governments also catalog their purchasable reports.

Indexes. Indexes to periodicals provide alphabetical lists of articles arranged by author and topic. The most widely available is the *Reader's Guide to Periodical Literature,* which indexes all the articles appearing in approximately one hundred mass-circulation magazines. More specialized indexes include the *Agricultural Index, Applied Science and Technology Index, Education Index, International Index: A Guide to Periodical Literature in the Social Sciences and the Humanities,* and *Public Affairs Information Service.* These list articles appearing in professional and scholarly journals.

Indexes to major newspapers also exist. Most libraries contain the *New York Times Index,* which lists (by topic) the articles that have appeared in the newspaper during a given year. Major collections also contain indexes for the *Christian Science Monitor, Wall Street Journal* and the London *Times.*

Professional journals. As a discipline, public administration boasts a wealth of professional journals. The list of potentially useful titles is so long that it would take a pamphlet (at least) simply to contain them. Here we can only give a brief glimpse at what is available.

Journals fall into three categories. First, there are those which cover the entire discipline, e.g., *Public Administration Review, International Journal of Public Administration, Southern Journal of Public Administration,* and the *Bureaucrat.*

Second, there are journals specializing in a particular administrative activity. Examples are *Public Personnel Management,* which concentrates on the personnel function, and *Training and Development Journal,* which focusses on training and organizational development.

Third, many journals specialize in a particular substantive field. For example, *Urban Education, Urban Review, Peabody Journal of Education, Educational Administration Quarterly,* and *Education and Urban Society* focus on educational administration. The *Journal of Police Science and Administration*, *Police Studies*, and the *Criminal Justice Review* contain articles on law enforcement.

The list of potential fields is virtually endless. A report writer consults relevant indexes to ascertain what has been written on a given subject.

Professional texts. Keeping up with professional texts is at least as difficult as remaining abreast of the journal literature. It sometimes seems as if new titles are published every day. Reading book reviews in professional journals is a good way of noting interesting new titles and holding them in mind for future reference. Also, the *Public Administration Times* (a professional newspaper)[7] summarizes new works of interest.

Some agency libraries provide literature updates for their administrators. At the Port Authority of New York and New Jersey, an administrator can ask for an update on a topic such as "Women in Management" and receive a computer printout listing recent books and articles.

READING AND TAKING NOTES

To use secondary sources properly, administrators have to know how to take notes. Luckily, this is a skill that improves with practice, the trick being to avoid both the extremes of writing too much or too little. (Jot down every idea and you go home with pages of irrelevancies; write too little and you may not be able to decipher the few words you do record.)

Different notetaking systems work best for different people. Some administrators take notes on three-by-five-inch index cards which permits shuffling and rearranging when the time comes to structure the information. Others use looseleaf notebooks which are easy to carry between the office and library. Try each system two or three times and see which works best for you.

Success at taking notes depends on an administrator's ability to extract information quickly from printed sources. This, in turn, depends on the ability to read intelligently, which means the reader should:

1. Glance through the entire book or article before beginning to take notes.

2. Examine a book's preface, abstract, table of contents and summary to get a general idea of the material.

3. Concentrate on the first and last paragraphs of chapters; authors use them to announce and summarize ideas. Pay attention to headings and italicized material.

4. Only record relevant points, material that you can use.

5. Use the simplest language possible.

6. Write clearly. Remember that you have to be able to understand the material in order to put it to use.

OUTLINING

Once information is collected, it must be arranged into categories. Outlines (rough schemes for writing papers) are an aid for deciding what the order of presentation should be. They show the relationships among various pieces of information and help identify a logical sequence. Once you have a workable outline, the actual task of writing the paper becomes a bit easier. (One reason so many people find writing difficult is that they try to write without first organizing their thoughts in an outline.)

Format

A number of outlining systems exist, but the most widely followed format is:

I.   Major topic
   A.   Principal idea
      1.   Secondary idea
         a.   Third-level idea
            i.   Fourth-level idea

We can use this format to construct a sample outline, assuming that we have an assignment to write an inhouse paper on energy policy and we have already collected our information.

I.   Establishing an energy policy.
   A.   The problem.
      1.   Current waste.
      2.   Increasing pollution.
   B.   The approach.

1. Serious conservation commitment.
2. Application of innovative technologies.

II. Strategies for Energy Development.
   A. Development of indigenous resources.
      1. Rationale.
         a. Independence from foreign suppliers.
         b. Employment opportunities for American workers.
      2. Likely sources.
         a. Wastes.
            i. Refuse.
            ii. Other.
         b. Forest products.
         c. Solar energy.
         d. Wind energy.
         e. Geothermal energy.
         f. Nuclear energy.
         g. Ocean thermal gradient.
   B. Creation of Energy Research and Development Office.

Notice that in the sample outline items are grouped according to the logical development of the argument. First, section I gives an overview of the need for and approach to creating an energy policy. The writer identifies the problem of waste and pollution and offers a generic approach involving a commitment to conservation and the application of new technologies. Then, section II identifies two strategies to implement this approach. One is to develop native American resources and the other is to create an agency that will promote energy-related research and development.

At all times, similar items are given similar weight. Thus, development of indigenous resources and creation of an Energy Research and Development Office are separate, comparable strategies so both are identified as principal ideas.

All items at any given level are written in parallel grammatical form (generally as nouns, verbs, or phrases) and approximately equal in length. Logical development and parallel construction make an outline easy to follow. The person writing the report has a good idea what information to place at each point.

CONCLUSIONS

In report writing, completion of the outline marks the end of the preparatory stage. Requisite information has been collected; basic structure is set. Of course, the structure and organization of a report may be altered at any time during the writing and rewriting stages, as ideas change or become clearer in the act of composition. But with the outline as a guide the writer is ready to begin writing.

Literally thousands of communications are written each day in public agencies and their form and content vary enormously. No book could possibly give detailed, specific rules for writing all of them. In this and the following chapter, we analyze *basic* strategies for presenting information. The emphasis is on pulling a paper together so that it actually reaches its audience and achieves its aims.

15

Presenting Information: Content and Style

Memoranda, summaries, option papers, position papers, progress reports, and training manuals are all important vehicles of agency communication. This chapter analyzes guidelines for preparing all of them. We identify the situations in which each is appropriate and explore how to develop, construct, and present the various formats. At all times, our analysis builds on the strategies for collecting and organizing information we described in the previous chapter.

MEMORANDA

The memorandum is the most commonly used written communication. It is unlikely that the most diligent search could uncover a single senior administrator who has not used memoranda many times as directives (to transmit decisions) and records (of meetings and other interactions). Most public administrators send memoranda regularly to their superiors, their peers, and their subordinates. They use memoranda as a record of day-to-day events and as evidence of decisions taken, options employed.

Because memoranda are so pervasive, many go unread. Those that are read are often misunderstood or fail to inspire action. When a memorandum goes unread or unheeded, the fault generally lies with the communicator. He or she writes without giving enough thought to the audience's needs and values and pays too little attention to proper memorandum content and style.

You can identify the qualities of an effective memorandum by performing a simple test. Collect ten agency memoranda.[1] Divide the lot into those you consider "effective" and "ineffective." Ask yourself: Why are some memoranda effective? What qualities make them successful? Why are some ineffective? What makes me think I would disregard them if they were sent to me in an agency? You are likely to find that the following points contribute to effectiveness.

1. Logical structure. Successful memoranda have a logical structure, including a brief introduction, discussion (focussing on one central point), and conclusion, emphasizing the major idea.

The writer concentrates on the main concerns of the message without sidetracking. Ideas flow logically. Evidence, arguments, and assertions are all relevant to the discussion at hand.

2. Brevity. Good memoranda are kept as brief as possible. Some administrators place a one-page limit on those they send but this is an arbitrary maximum. The important point is to weed out repetitions and prune cumbersome phrases. Often one word says as much as three or four, e.g., by rather than by means of, if rather than in the event of. Always reread first drafts and cut where necessary.

3. Clarity. Adjust the language to the audience. Use words and phrases that your readers understand.

4. Action-orientation. If the memorandum contains a directive, make action easy by explicitly identifying what you want done and assigning a specific deadline, wherever possible.

Figure 15.1 is a simulated action-oriented memorandum written by a department chairperson at a state university. Notice that the communicator opens by explaining the purpose of the request, thus motivating compliance. The second paragraph

FIG. 15.1. SAMPLE MEMORANDUM

To: Professor Mary Smith
From: Professor John Henrique
Subject: Self-Evaluation Assignments
Date: October 12, 1982

Our yearly process of departmental self-assessment is currently underway. One of the tasks facing us is evaluating all of the undergraduate courses taught in our department, and I would like your input for the courses you are teaching—Introduction to Public Administration and Public Budgeting.

Specifically, we need the following information:
1. Objectives of each course,
2. Current textbook(s) used, and
3. Course outline(s).

Since time is of the essence, the deadline for submission is October 30, 1982. If you have any questions, feel free to consult with me or others who have taught the course. Thank you for your cooperation.

describes the assignment specifically and identifies a deadline. Even though the request is quite brief and clear, the communicator urges the recipient to contact him (or others) if there are any questions.

SUMMARIES

It is difficult for any administrator to digest all the reports and articles relating to his or her work. In order to keep abreast, officials ask their subordinates to prepare summaries of important written or oral presentations.

Effective summaries are:
1. Brief: appropriate length is generally one page or less.
2. Inclusive: all major points appearing in the original document must be included.
3. Logical: equal ideas are treated equally. The writer

identifies all major points in logical order; sub-topics follow the major point to which they pertain.

4. Clear: the writer uses words and phrases with which the audience is familiar. Technical terms (argot and jargon) are reserved for specialized audiences.

5. Accurate: a summary should only contain ideas which appear in the work being summarized. The writer never offers his own analysis, even if he disagrees wholeheartedly with the original communication. He concentrates on describing points quickly and accurately so that the audience receives a useful overview of a particular document. A summary offers exactly what its name implies—a shortened version of ideas expressed in another presentation.

Options Papers

Options papers examine the alternatives that are available to an administrator in a given situation. When senior officials have a decision to make, they often need an impartial analysis of their options. Accordingly, they ask their assistants to prepare a report identifying plausible actions and forecasting the consequences (advantages and disadvantages) of each.

Options papers are analyses not recommendations. The writer concentrates on identifying a diverse set of alternatives and performing the same type of analysis on each, describing the benefits and dysfunctions of every choice without advocating any one alternative over the others. The objective is to generate a sufficiently varied set of choices and subject them to an analysis with enough depth and rigor to be of use to the decision maker.

The worth of an options paper depends on its structure, clarity, and depth of analysis. The writer strives for logical organization, readable format, and valid, sufficient evidence to support assertions.

Logical Organization

An options paper begins with a brief description of a policy dilemma including its background and causes. The rest of the paper analyzes alternative arrangements for solving the problem and the advantages and disadvantages of using each.

A logical structure for such a paper is:
I.   Background.
     A. Organizational setting.
     B. Problem.
         1. Causes.
         2. Consequences.
II. First Alternative.
     A. Description.
     B. Advantages.
     C. Disadvantages.
III. Second Alternative.
     A. Description.
     B. Advantages.
     C. Disadvantages. . .

Readable Format

Keep the format clear and easy to follow. Use titles and headings to demarcate sections; let the reader know when one analysis ends and a second begins. Use the same format throughout the paper. Decide beforehand how to handle transitions between sections and stick to the prearranged method. (A sample format appears in the Appendix.)

Valid, Sufficient Evidence

Since the goal of an options paper is thorough analysis, all arguments must be backed with valid (relevant) and sufficient evidence. For example, assume an administrator writes a paper on educational funding. She supports the statement, "College graduates earn more money than high school graduates," with evidence on the average earnings of college and high school graduates. If the point were that high school graduates earn less than $20,000, then a statement about *their* average earnings would be sufficient. If the point were that high school graduates are unhappy about their low incomes, then the writer might use an opinion survey as support. In either case, the writer chooses the pertinent evidence to prove her point.

In researching options papers administrators must be familiar with all the sources described in the last chapter. Amassing and analyzing a diverse set of alternatives can require an extensive literature search, astute personal observation, interviewing, and the use of a survey questionnaire.

POSITION PAPERS

Position papers advocate a particular solution to a given policy dilemma. The writer identifies a problem and then argues the merits of one approach from what may be a wide universe of plausible choices.

Unlike an options paper, the position paper seeks to persuade, not to offer an impartial analysis. Accordingly, the writer marshalls a wide variety of data—historical, political, philosophical, and statistical—that support one position and arranges them in a manner calculated to convince others that this choice is right.

Two logical formats for this are the problem-solution and causal structures as discussed in chapter 9. A position paper's opening section identifies the problem, exploring its causes and consequences. The rest of the paper argues the merits of the solution that the writer favors.

PROGRESS REPORTS

Progress reports are documents that describe ongoing activities. Most identify an agency or unit's goals and objectives, accomplishments, problems encountered, solutions tried, and the need (if any) to revise plans. Thus the progress report is an instrument of hierarchical control. It travels up the chain of command, giving senior officials necessary information on an agency's performance and the measures they must take to overcome any deficiencies. A well-written report facilitates planning, evaluation, and control.

Types of Reports

Several types of progress reports exist, each intended for a somewhat different audience. Junior administrators prepare daily, weekly, monthly, and quarterly reports meant for internal consumption. These reports contain extensive detail on past, current, and projected activities within a single bureau or section.

They serve as a link between the units and top management, helping commissioners and cabinet secretaries keep tabs on what occurs at the operating level.

Top officials oversee the preparation of monthly, quarterly, and annual reports which are sent to the chief executive (mayor, governor, or president) and the legislature. These papers give an overview of activities in the entire agency. They serve as a link between the bureaucratic and political worlds, and thus help keep the agency accountable to democratically elected authorities.

As an example of this diversity let us look at New York City's management reporting system, which operates on three distinct levels: agency, executive, and mayoral.[2]

Throughout the year, bureau chiefs in each organization send frequent *agency reports* to their commissioners. These papers contain a high level of detail on the unit:

1. Workload—operational responsibilities (e.g., miles of street to be swept).

2. Output—work accomplished (e.g., miles of street actually swept).

3. Efficiency—a productivity indicator expressed as a ratio between work accomplished and resources applied (e.g., miles of street swept per hours worked per sanitation worker).

4. Effectiveness—impact of the tasks performed on the quality of city life (e.g., citizen ratings of street cleanliness).

Once a month, each commissioner sends an *executive report* to the mayor. These reports are prepared by analysts on the commissioner's staff using the data collected by the bureau chiefs. (Ideally, they contain the most important data. However, at this stage, a problem of status distortion sometimes does emerge and commissioners play down problems in their bailiwicks, preferring to focus on areas where goals are being met.[3])

Every February and August, the mayor sends a report to the City Council and the Board of Estimate. Because this report deals with over thirty agencies, it contains the fewest details. The text highlights key performance indicators and the most significant findings on each agency's management. The legislators use this information in budgeting and allocating funds.

Style and Content

Whatever their audience, effective progress reports depend on an honest, constructive tone and a format so clear that people unfamiliar with a given unit can follow a description of its activities without any difficulty. The subsections below examine how such tone and format are produced.

Honest, constructive tone. Honest reports are the only ones of any use. If a unit suffers a major performance setback, the writer reports it and gives ample consideration to causes and effects.

Release of information on major deficiencies may easily promote cynicism unless the writer adds an analysis of what may be done to improve performance.[4] Any material on setbacks should be followed with recommendations for change with the writer explaining the need for and use of a particular remedy. Figure 15.2 gives an example of honest, constructive tone in a social service agency report. The writer acknowledges a problem with incorrect reporting of welfare client income, describes what the agency is doing to alleviate the problem, and suggests additional remedies.

Clear Format. The organization of progress reports is relatively straightforward. They begin with a title page, which contains the name of the report, the date, and the person for whom it is intended. A letter of transmittal follows when the report is sent outside the agency. (Figure 15.3 is a sample letter.) Longer reports (ca. twenty or more pages) generally have a table of contents to orient the readers. An overview (or summary) is also useful.

The body of the report is organized by activity. Each section identifies clearly and specifically the progress that has been made in a particular area, what problems remain (if any), and the need for possible solutions.

Progress reports often contain tables, charts, graphs, and statistical maps, because the analysis requires statistical indicators (manpower allocations, cost figures, etc.). Pictorial aids help readers grasp this kind of information quickly (see chapter 16).

FIG. 15.2. IMPROVED WELFARE ADMINISTRATION

—*Incorrect reporting of income.* Approximately one third of all overpayments are related to income, in cases such as the client's failure to report employment earnings or the incorrect reporting of outside income. . . .

The State had achieved major inroads against payments to ineligible persons and overpayments during 1973 through the overhaul of initial eligibility . . . to require more accurate client documentation of need. Department auditors had discovered that most eligibility and overpayment errors occurred within 90 days after the recipient was admitted to the welfare rolls and to counteract this the Department instituted periodic face-to-face recertification interviews requiring recipients to verify their continued need for assistance.

During 1974 the Department evaluated additional measures to augment the effectiveness of the recertification interview, including:

—Expanded requirements for home visits to validate client assertions. . . .

—More penetrating interview techniques aimed at problem areas such as unreported bank accounts. . . .

—Impressing clients with their responsibility to report all information pertaining to their eligibility and outside income.

Source: New York State Department of Social Services, *The Annual Report of the New York State Department of Social Services* (Albany, 1974), pp. 5-6.

In short, keep the format attractive and simple. Let coherent organization and mode of presentation help convey analysis. Always remember that the reader knows less about the activities of any single unit than the administrator who collects the data.

TRAINING MANUALS

Training manuals are basic sources of information about agency policies and procedures. Used in orientation and on-the-job instruction, they are among the first communications a new administrator encounters and often set the tone for information exchange in the agency.

Effective training manuals are relatively difficult to produce because old and new administrators view policies and procedures from different perspectives. Handbook writers are so familiar with the agency practices that they tend to proceed quickly and use the latest jargon.

Newcomers are unfamiliar with the way things are handled in a particular department. They do not understand the organization's latest "buzz" words. They need a simple, clear, step-by-step outline of tasks and responsibilities.

FIG. 15.3. SAMPLE LETTER

Honorable Hugh L. Carey, Governor,
State of New York

Honorable Brendan T. Byrne, Governor,
State of New Jersey

April 12, 1979

Your Excellencies:

In accordance with the Port Compact of 1921, we are pleased to submit to you and to the Legislatures of the States of New York and New Jersey the 1978 Annual Report of the Port Authority of New York and New Jersey.

Respectfully yours,

Alan Sagner   Robert F. Wagner
Chairman   Vice Chairman

Source: Port Authority of New York and New Jersey, 1978 Annual Report, p. 1.

Manual writers thus have to be able to put themselves in the new administrator's shoes. It is not enough for them to write in a style the novice might understand. They must learn to write in a way that encourages the new administrator to turn to the manual whenever a question arises.

The key to successful writing is to make information easy to find and assimilate. Training manuals are no place for argot or gobbledygook; technical terms should be kept to a minimum. Lists are useful because the numbers and short paragraphs make items easy to find. (The same holds for colored tabs and headings demarcating sections.)

The writer should begin each explanation with a paragraph on purpose, thereby motivating the readers and making them as eager as possible to get additional information. Summaries, which remind people what they have already learned, are another potential motivator.

Effective use can be made of graphic and visual techniques, including:

1. flowcharts to help readers visualize processes;

2. tables, charts, and graphs for statistical data; and

3. diagrams and photographs of equipment and operating procedures.

To sum up: always aim your product at the least experienced person using it. Present material in a format that even he has no problem understanding.

CONCLUSION

While the formats discussed in this chapter vary greatly in purpose and potential audience, several common characteristics emerge. Whether written material flows up or down the chain of command (or between peer departments), it should always be simple, clear, well-organized, and attractively packaged. To teach effective written communication, we need only paraphrase the Golden Rule: Write for others as you would have others write for you.

16

Presenting Statistical Information

Many of the papers we discussed in the last chapter require the use of statistical data. Numbers are such an invaluable aid to recording performance that it is rare to see options papers, position papers, and progress reports without some statistical analysis. A rudimentary background in collecting, analyzing, and presenting numerical data is almost a prerequisite today for both writing and reading public agency documents.

USING AND MISUSING STATISTICS

Two types of statistics have a place in agency material: descriptive and inferential.

Descriptive Statistics

Descriptive statistics present and analyze numbers about complete populations. The average salary of a unit's employees or the average hours administrators work per year are examples of descriptive statistics because, in both cases, the agency keeps figures on all employees. To present the data, the writer need only add the figures and compute an average.

Descriptive statistics are tools for evaluation and control. They enable top managers to make comparisons over time and between units or agencies.

Statistical Inference

Statistical inference deals with data collected on a part of a population. The analyst collects data from a sample rather than the population as a whole either because it is impossible to contact the entire population or it is too expensive or time consuming to do so.

For example, assume the Internal Revenue Service wants information on the number of people who submit dishonest returns. No figures are kept on the exact size of this population. Revenue agents have to infer its size from the number of fraudulent returns they find in the relatively small sample they audit. Analysts in the agency review the sample in order to make inferences or draw conclusions about the size of the population.

Inferential statistics is a planning tool. Given a set of proposed actions and a set of outcomes associated with each action, statisticians can often report the probability that each outcome will occur. This helps administrators choose among conflicting options.

Misusing Statistics

Mark Twain once said that there were lies, damn lies, and then statistics. In an age where many people readily intone, "Figures don't lie," it is important to add "But liars can figure." The administrator should be on guard against deliberate and accidental misuses of statistics. The subsections below examine three such misleading practices.

Inaccurate representation of underlying facts. Administrators who use inferential statistics should have some idea of how the numbers are collected in the first place. A sample tells you nothing about the population as a whole if the sample itself is skewed or too small. (You cannot learn how the entire American nation votes if you limit your sample to registered Republicans or ten of your closest friends.)

Data based on questionnaires often suffer from inaccurate representation. Many recipients fail to reply. Those who do generally possess some characteristic (deep interest in the topic, a high sense of commitment, etc.) that distinguishes them and makes their replies a poor indicator of the whole population.

Administrators who use inferential statistics must remember that sample data only reflect the population when the sample itself is sufficient and representative. Thus it is important only to rely on data when you have some idea how the numbers were collected in the first place.

Confusing Association and Causation. Statistical research constantly uncovers relationships among variables. But some people assume that any correlation automatically indicates that one variable causes the other. By thus inferring causation from association they ignore the possibility that the relationship may be a coincidence or that a third variable may cause both of the first two.

For example, the available data indicate a correlation between increased schooling and higher lifetime income. But this does not necessarily mean the fact of staying in school *causes* people to earn more money. Those who finish degree programs or go on to professional schools may come from a higher socio-economic background than those who do not, and this may account for their having high income jobs.

Carelessness. Most people take for granted that professionals compute figures accurately. Unfortunately, even statisticians sometimes make mistakes from arithmetical carelessness.

If an administrator prepares a report and crucial figures seem out of line, he or she can contact the people who compiled or processed the underlying data. They may be willing to review their arithmetic if they cannot explain the alleged discrepancy.

Effective Presentation

While agencies collect and organize numbers every minute of the day, many administrators still feel uncomfortable using statistical data. Report writers have to make a special effort to present numbers in a form that managers find relatively easy and painless to assimilate. This section analyzes three possible methods of presentation. The aim is to give readers an idea of the advantages and disdvantages of each so that they can choose the most appropriate style in a given situation.

Text

The presentation of statistics in the text, especially if there are many figures, is generally ineffective. Lacking visual cues to clarify and interpret relationships, the reader may not understand the meaning of isolated figures. Most people find it easier to abstract numerical information from tables, charts, and graphs than from textual narrative.

Tables

Tables are logically structured arrangements of figures in columns and horizontal lines. Clues to interpretation are carried by the title of the table and by suitable phrases above the columns identifying the different elements of data. Tables serve as effective visual aids, because they facilitate analysis and comparison. Figures 16.1 and 16.2 present the same housing data in textual and tabular form. Notice how much clearer the table is and how much easier it is to find any particular number.

Tables are relatively easy to construct. Here are five pointers.

Keep titles brief and clear. Every table needs a brief title which is complete enough to give readers an overview of the contents without being longwinded or tedious to read. In general, restrict the length to a single phrase or sentence.

FIG. 16.1. TRENDS IN OVERCROWDED HOUSING

In 1940, 9.0% of all households had more than 1.5 persons per room. In 1950, 6.2% of all households had 1.5 persons per room. In 1960, the figure was 3.6% of all the households. In 1970, it was 2.0%. In 1976, 1.0% of all households had more than 1.5 persons per room.

Source: Congress of the United States, Congressional Budget Office, *Federal Housing Policy: Current Programs and Recurring Issues* (Washington, D.C.: U.S. Government Printing Office, 1978), p. 9.

Indicate sources.   Indicate the source of the data in a footnote at the bottom of the table. Unless you have collected the information yourself, you must identify all sources (see figure 16.2).

List items in meaningful order.   Arrange data in the way that makes it easiest for your readers to locate particular elements. Let the subject matter dictate which pattern you use. In a historical overview, try chronological columns. In a table giving data on the fifty states, use an alphabetical listing. For some tables, it is best to arrange the numbers according to a characteristic of the data itself (e.g., per capita income, population density). The columns in figure 16.2 are arranged in chronological order; the horizontal rows are arranged according to a characteristic of the data.

Emphasize important items.   In some tables, one or two entries are crucial. Emphasize these by putting them in the top line or the extreme right- or left-hand column where they are easiest to see. Underlining a particular entry or using a special typeface also rivets attention.

Place tables for maximum impact.   Tables come in two varieties. Summary tables, which present a few closely related findings, belong in the body of the report near the text they illuminate. (Figure 16.2 is a summary table.) Reference tables of

FIG. 16.2. TRENDS IN OVERCROWDED HOUSING, 1940-1976

Criteria of Overcrowding	Percent of Households				
	1940	1950	1960	1970	1976
More than 1.5 Persons Per Room	9.0	6.2	3.6	2.0	1.0
More than 1.0 Person Per Room	20.3	15.7	11.5	8.0	4.6

Source: Congress of the United States, Congressional Budget Office, *Federal Housing Policy: Current Programs and Recurring Issues* (Washington, D.C.: U.S. Government Printing Office, 1978), p. 9.

several pages, which store large quantities of data, are too long and involved to place in the body of the report. They belong in an appendix at the end.

Graphs and Charts

Graphs and charts are visual devices that often appear in agency reports. They show relationships among variables at a glance. They are easier to analyze than tables (particularly when the tables are long and bulky.) They relieve reader monotony by imparting an attractive, eye-catching look to the page.

But graphs and charts have two limitations. First, you can present more information in a table than in a graph or chart; visual aids are only useful as substitutes for summary (rather than reference) tables. Second, elaborate charts and graphs take a lot of time to produce. Each report writer has to decide whether the additional expenditure of time is justified in terms of lightening the reader's load. When junior administrators prepare a report for top management (or chief executives and legislatures), the effort often is justified.

Graphs. In graphs, statistical data are plotted in reference to a pair of intercepting lines called *axes*. The horizontal line is the X axis or *ordinate*; the vertical line is the Y axis or *abscissa*. The spot where the two lines intersect is known as the *point of origin*; the value of this point must be zero on at least one axis.

Graphs are excellent devices for diagramming ratios and frequency distributions. They allow the communicator to express complex relationships in a compressed form (see figure 16.3).

Most rules for writing tables apply to graphs as well. Brief, clear titles are necessary. (They may be placed over the figure—just like the title of a table—or below it.) Footnotes are used to indicate outside sources. In addition, graphs require labels for the X and Y axes. Generally, we place the label for the X axis underneath the body of the graph, the label for the Y axis on top of the highest number in the left-hand column.

Bar Charts. A bar chart (or graph) uses colored bars to show frequency distributions. The magnitude of the bars indicates the relative sizes of different data categories. There are two types of bar charts: vertical (figure 16.4) and horizontal (figure 16.5). The

Ratio of
Nonwhite to White

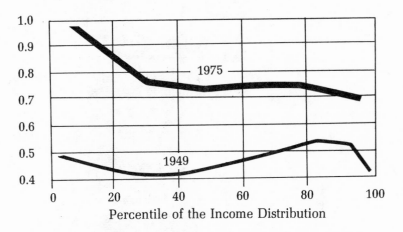

Percentile of the Income Distribution

FIG. 16.3. RATIOS OF NONWHITE-TO-WHITE
INCOME TO PERSONS, 1949 AND 1975

Source: Congressional Budget Office, *Income Disparities between Black and White Americans* (Washington, D.C.: U.S. Government Printing Office, 1977), p. 9.

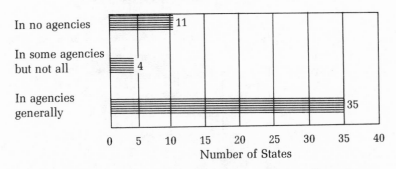

FIG. 16.5. NUMBER OF STATES HAVING OFFICIAL POLICY OR
FORMAL STATEMENT ON LABOR-MANAGEMENT RELATIONS

Source: United States Civil Service Commission, Bureau of Intergovernmental Personnel Programs, *Conference Report on Public Personnel Management Reform* (Washington, D.C., January 1978), back cover.

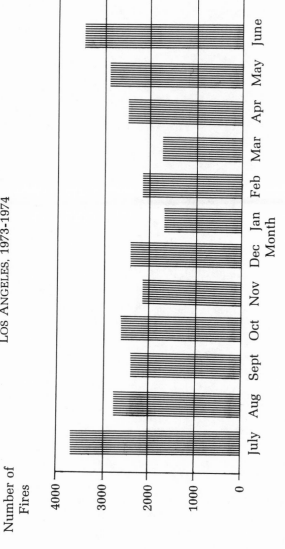

FIG. 16.4. FIRE FREQUENCY BY MONTH:
LOS ANGELES, 1973-1974

Source: Los Angeles City Fire Department, *Statistical Report, 1973-74*, p. 3.

more common vertical form is generally used to compare data over time. The horizontal format lends itself to geographical comparisons. In both, at least one axis always starts at zero.

Pie Charts. A pie chart is a circular diagram whose circumference represents 100 percent of a given entity and whose interior shows that entity's component parts (see figure 16.6).

Public managers often need to answer questions that involve proportions and percentages. (What proportion of college graduates become teachers? What percentage of families live in substandard housing?) The pie chart is an appropriate visual tool for answering such questions because it emphasizes relative size of components and both their relation to each other and the entire diagram.

To make a pie chart, you draw a circle that represents some total entity. (The size of the diameter depends on the space available and the overall design.) Then you apportion the components using a protractor that divides the circle into one

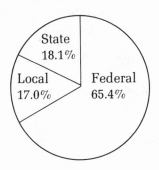

FIG. 16.6. TAX REVENUES FROM FEDERAL, STATE AND
LOCAL GOVERNMENTS AS A PERCENT OF
TOTAL TAX REVENUE, 1966/67

Source: U.S. Bureau of the Census, *U.S. Census of Governments: 1967, Vol. VI, No. 5: Historical Statistics on Government Finances and Employment* (Washington, D.C.: U.S. Government Printing Office, 1967).

hundred equal parts. (This lets you know what percent of the whole any angle represents.) Draw the first radius vertically from the center, arranging the remaining components in a clockwise order. Finish by providing each part with a brief clear label and the chart itself with an appropriate title.

Pictographs. Pictographs are graphs that use small pictures to represent data. For example, an administrator may use stick figures to symbolize an agency's clients or dollar signs to represent a unit's budget. Each symbol stands for a specified number of items. Thus, if one $ stands for 100,000 dollars, then the pictograph

1970	$
1980	$$

indicates that a particular department's budget rose from 100,000 dollars in 1970 to 200,000 dollars in 1980.

Pictographs enjoyed a vogue before World War II because they relieve monotony. Today, their use has declined; bar graphs are both easier to construct and more suitable for handling complex data. (For example, a pictograph could not handle the information presented in figure 16.4.)

Statistical Maps. A statistical map shows quantitative relationships geographically. The writer shades specific areas of the map to indicate how the data vary in different locales. A legend is provided to show what the various colors, dots, stripes, hatches, etc., mean (see figure 16.7).

Maps command attention. Their chief advantage is that they are striking. However, maps are relatively difficult to construct and cost more to produce than most other charts and graphs. The writer must decide whether the purpose of the communication justifies the additional expense.

CONCLUSIONS

Understand your purpose in presenting information. This is an appropriate maxim to conclude this chapter (and the unit) because the inextricable relationship between purpose and strategy is the single most crucial concept that the public agency communicator masters. You cannot choose an effective style for

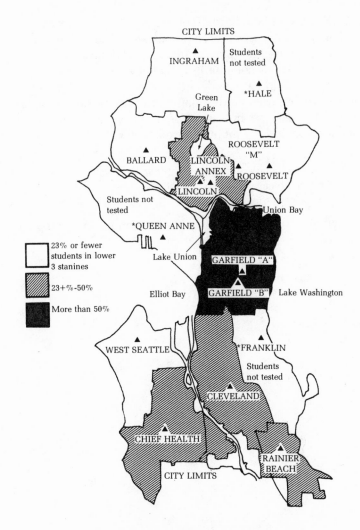

FIG. 16.7. LOW ACHIEVING STUDENTS
IN SEATTLE HIGH SCHOOLS
BASED ON COMBINED VERBAL AND
NUMERICAL ABILITIES TESTS

Source: Seattle Public Schools, *Needs Assessment for State U.R.R.D. Funded Programs in Seattle* (January, 1975), p. 14.

statistical presentation until you have decided on how that data furthers your goal. In every communication issue analyzed in this volume, purpose determines effective style and content.

Effective agency communicators always know the goal of each message they initiate and choose strategies that bring them towards their particular destination. Otherwise, both writers and readers can get lost in a maze of unrelated data. Alice, lost in Wonderland, has the following exchange with the Cheshire cat:

> "Would you tell me, please, which way I ought to go from here?"
> "That depends on where you want to get to," said the Cat.
> "I don't much care where . . ." said Alice.
> "Then it doesn't matter which way you go," said the Cat.[1]

First know your objective when you communicate. Then plan the best approach for reaching that goal.

Summing Up
Concepts for Review;
Problems and Exercises

Bar charts
Pie charts
Pictographs
Statistical maps

PROBLEMS AND EXERCISES

1. In a local social service agency, caseworkers used hospital records to check paternity in family-aid cases. The unit chief felt this practice was unreliable because many hospitals list any man identified by the mother, even if he disclaims paternity. The chief, therefore, wrote the following memorandum to all caseworkers.

From: John Garibaldi, Unit Chief
To: All Caseworkers
Re: Checking Paternity
Date: March 30, 1980
Effective April 1, no worker is to check paternity by using hospital records.

   a. Criticize John Garibaldi's memo.
   b. Rewrite the entire memorandum to increase its effectiveness.

2. Obtain a training manual or handbook from an agency in your area.

   a. Criticize its strengths and weaknesses.
   b. Choose a one to three page section which you feel needs revision. Rewrite that section to increase its effectiveness as a training tool. Explain in one or two paragraphs why you made each revision to the original text. Use such criteria as audience needs and values, readability, attractive format, etc.

3. Select a public-policy problem that interests you and assume that you work as an administrator in the agency responsible for its solution.

   a. Write a fifteen to twenty page options paper analyzing at least two alternative solutions your agency can implement. Explain the advantages and disadvantages of each. Bring evidence to support general statements of fact, assertions, and inferences.

b. Assume the commissioner of your agency decides to implement one of the solutions you analyzed in the options paper. Write a ten to fifteen page position paper advocating that particular solution. (You choose the lucky option.)

c. What similarities of style and content exist between your options and position papers? What differences do you see?

d. Prepare a one-page summary of your options or position paper.

4. Read the paragraph below from the Bigtown Police Department's *Annual Report*. Comment on the writer's use of evidence.

For several years, Bigtown has been plagued with high crime rates in public housing projects. In 1979, the Bigtown Police Department assigned 1,110 police officers to public housing projects. In 1980, we doubled this figure. (By using one-officer patrol cars in other areas, we freed officers for housing project duty.)

We are happy to report that crime is now down at Bigtown's housing projects. There were 6,548 housing project felonies committed in 1979 and only 4,200 in 1980. We can definitely attribute the decrease in crime in our city to the new police program.

5. Assume you work in the personnel department of a public works agency. Recently, the training division established a series of offsite leadership workshops for professional employees. Your unit's assignment is to prepare an evaluation report on the workshops.

a. List three sources you might consult to get information for the report.

b. Explain the advantages and disadvantages of using each source.

6. Read the following paragraph.

Our agency employs 14,698 people in all titles: 1,450 are managers, 10,500 are line employees, and the others work in staff capacities. For line operations, we divide the city into five subareas. Subarea A is 70 square miles and has a population of 2,602,012. Subarea B has an area of 108 square miles and a population of 1,987,174. Subarea C has a population of 1,539,233 and an area of 23 square miles. Subarea D has an area of 41 square miles and subarea E has one of 58 square miles. The population of subarea D is 1,471,701, and of the last subarea, 295,443.

a. Prepare a table or tables that present the information in a clear, concise, easy-to-read manner.
b. Prepare a chart that illustrates the variation in physical size among the five subareas.

APPENDIX
Sample Options Paper

This selection illustrates one format for handling the description and analysis of alternatives in an options paper. It originally appeared in the Congressional Budget Office, *The Long-Term Costs of Lower-Income Housing Assistance Programs* (Washington, D.C.: U.S. Government Printing Office, 1979), pp. 51–55. Since U.S. Congress members are a principal audience for this paper, the language is fairly sophisticated and aimed at readers with indepth knowledge of the policy process.

REDUCING OVERALL HOUSING ASSISTANCE COSTS

Options for reducing the costs of all current housing assistance programs include:
- Increase the reliance on existing housing;
- Increase the share of income that tenants are required to pay in rent; and
- Alter the mix of tenants to serve persons with higher incomes.

Increase the Reliance on Existing Housing

Because of the substantial difference in rents between new and existing housing, housing assistance costs could be reduced appreciably by directing a larger share of all housing aid to programs that make use of the existing rental stock. In recent years, however, the trend has been towards less, rather than more, existing housing assistance. In fiscal year 1977, the Section 8 existing housing program and the purchase of existing, standard units for use as public housing accounted for 48 percent of all new subsidy commitments. During the next year, the rate dropped to 45 percent. HUD's original budget submission for fiscal year 1979 called for 41 percent of the additional commitments to be made through the Section 8 existing housing program and for no further direct purchases of existing standard units for public housing. The most recent operating plan for fiscal year 1979 and HUD budget submission for 1980 call for 34 percent of all commitments to be for Section 8 existing housing. By shifting the emphasis from new construction to existing housing, more persons could be assisted at a lower total cost to the federal government. Because of the shorter lead time needed to lease existing units, however, a move toward more existing housing assistance would actually increase federal outlays for the first few years after the commitments are made.

Although increasing the reliance on existing housing assistance would reduce long-term costs, it might also diminish the effect of housing assistance programs on the supply of decent housing. Because the Section 8 new construction/substantial rehabilitation program provides an owner with a partial guarantee of rental income, it may encourage the development of housing that would not otherwise have been built. It may, on the other hand, merely substitute subsidized for unsubsidized housing. Since it pays the development and financing costs for publicly owned housing, the public housing program also adds to the supply of new units—provided, again, that the federally financed construction does not merely substitute for development that would have occurred in any event. By contrast, the Section 8 existing housing program does not induce new construction. Existing housing assistance does, however, result in some upgrading of marginally substandard units and may contribute to long-term maintenance. It is not clear from available evidence whether the net addition to the supply of decent housing that occurs through new construction programs exceeds the net impact of the upgrading and improving maintenance resulting from existing housing assistance.

Increase Tenant Rent Payments

The Congress could reduce federal outlays by increasing the share of income that tenants in assisted housing are required to pay toward their own housing expenses. For the past ten years, rental charges have been limited by law to no more than 25 percent of adjusted tenant income. The cost of housing assistance programs could be reduced significantly by raising the rental charges to a level above the current standard but still below what tenants would have to pay in the private market for comparable housing. Lower-income renters not receiving housing assistance are now paying an average of 39 percent of their incomes for housing, and fewer than one-fourth of all eligible renters now receive federal aid. By raising rent payments in assisted housing, the cost per household could be reduced and the proportion of the eligible population served could be increased, while still providing a substantial subsidy to those receiving aid. To alleviate the hardship that such a change might cause for the lowest-income families, a sliding scale of payments could be established, setting a lower rent-to-income standard for the poorest persons, while imposing somewhat higher rates on better-off tenants.

Smaller savings could be achieved by changing the rent rules in public housing to conform to those governing the Section 8 program. Such a change would reduce federal outlays for public housing operating subsidies and eliminate the disparity that now exists in the treatment of public housing and Section 8 tenants.

Alter the Mix of Tenants

A different approach to reduce the costs of rental assistance programs would be to require that they serve a larger number of persons with higher income. Because tenant rent payments in assisted housing are set at fixed percentages of family income, and because rent collections offset federal expenditures, higher average tenant incomes would result in lower costs to the government. With rental charges ranging from 15 to 25 percent of tenant incomes, every increase of $100 in the average annual tenant income would result in a savings to the government of between $15 and $25 per year for each unit of housing.

Increasing the proportion of higher-income tenants would also promote economic integration in assisted housing projects. It should be noted, however, that such economic integration is already encouraged under current law and regulations but has proven difficult to achieve. To the extent that HUD did succeed in shifting the tenant mix toward persons with higher incomes, the programs would then serve a greater number of families more likely to be able to afford decent housing in the unsubsidized market, to the exclusion of the lower-income families they would replace.

NOTES

Chapter 1: Setting Up and Maintaining Agency Communications

1. Alex Bavelas and D. Barrett, "An Experimental Approach to Organizational Communication," *Personnel*, 27 (1951), 366–71.

2. Charles R. Wright, *Mass Communication* (New York: Random House, 1959), p. 11.

3. For an overview of the communication process, see Wilbur Schramm, "How Communication Works," *The Process and Effects of Mass Communication*, edited by Wilbur Schramm (Urbana, Ill.: University of Illinois Press, 1965), pp. 3–26.

4. Herbert Simon, Donald Smithburg, and Victor Thompson, "The Communication Process," *Public Administration: Concepts and Cases*, edited by Richard J. Stillman II (Boston: Houghton Mifflin, 1976), pp. 177–83.

5. James Q. Wilson, "The Bureaucracy Problem," *Public Interest*, 6 (Winter 1967), 3–9.

6. Anthony Downs discusses the growth of informal channels in *Inside Bureaucracy* (Boston: Little, Brown, 1967), pp. 114–15.

7. See, for example, Paul Lazarsfeld, Bernard Berelson, and Hazel Gaudet, *The People's Choice* (New York: Columbia University Press, 1948) and Elihu Katz and Paul Lazarsfeld, *Personal Influence* (Glencoe, Ill.: Free Press, 1955).

Chapter 2: Communication and Informal Groups

1. Peter Blau, *Dynamics of Bureaucracy* (Chicago: University of Chicago Press, 1955), pp. 105-60.

2. Arnold E. Schneider, William C. Donaghy, and Pamela Jane Newman, *Organizational Communication* (New York: McGraw-Hill, 1975), p. 131.

3. Quoted in Studs Terkel, *Working* (New York: Pantheon Books, 1972), pp. 460-61.

4. Schneider, Donaghy, and Newman, *Organizational Communication*, p. 131.

5. This process is outlined in George Homans, *The Human Group* (New York: Harcourt, 1950), pp. 48-155.

6. Edwin Flippo, *Principles of Personnel Management*, 4th ed. (New York: McGraw-Hill, 1976), p. 412.

7. See, for example, George Strauss and Leonard R. Sayles, *Personnel: The Human Problems of Management*, 3d ed. (Englewood Cliffs, N.J.: Prentice-Hall, 1972), pp. 84-87.

8. Basil Wilson and John Cooper, "Ghetto Reflections and the Role of the Police Officer," *Journal of Police Science and Administration*, 7 (March 1979), 28-35.

9. William I. Bacchus, "Foreign Affairs Officials: Professionals without Professions?" *Public Administration Review*, 37 (November/December 1977), 641-50.

10. Henry P. Leifermann, "Mass Mutiny Aboard the U.S.S. Constellation," *Public Administration: Concepts and Cases*, edited by Richard J. Stillman II (Boston: Houghton Mifflin, 1976), pp. 112-19.

11. A noteworthy exception is Frederick C. Mosher and Richard J. Stillman II (eds.), "A Symposium: The Professions in Government," *Public Administration Review*, 37 (November/December 1977). Articles in this symposium supplied much of the background for this section.

12. Frederick C. Mosher and Richard J. Stillman II, "The Professions in Government: Introduction," *Public Administration Review*, 37 (November/December 1977), 631-33.

13. Peter Blau and W. Richard Scott, *Formal Organizations* (San Francisco: Chandler, 1962), p. 69.

14. See Frederick C. Mosher, *Democracy and the Public Service* (New York: Oxford University Press, 1968), pp. 103-33.

15. Stillman, *Public Administration: Concepts and Cases*, p. 122.

16. W. Henry Lambright and Albert H. Teich, "Scientists and Government: A Case of Professional Ambivalence," *Public Administration Review*, 38 (March/April 1978), 105-50.

17. Anthony Downs, *Inside Bureaucracy* (Boston: Little, Brown, 1967), p. 202.

18. Edward Shils, "Primary Groups in the American Army," *Continuities in Social Research,* edited by Robert K. Merton and Paul F. Lazarsfeld (New York: Free Press, 1950), pp. 16–39; and Edward Shils and Morris Janowitz, "Cohesion and Disintegration in the Wehrmacht in World War II," *The Process and Effects of Mass Communication,* edited by Wilbur Schramm (Urbana: University of Illinois Press, 1965), pp. 501–16.

19. Douglas M. McGregor, *The Human Side of Enterprise* (New York: McGraw-Hill, 1960), pp. 33–35.

20. Ibid.

21. Robert Hershey, "The Grapevine—Here to Stay But Not Beyond Control," *Personnel,* 43 (January/February 1966), 62–66.

22. Specific techniques for conducting staff meetings appear in chapter 13.

23. Quoted in John R. Russell, *Cases in Urban Management* (Cambridge, Mass.: MIT Press, 1974), p. 470.

24. Rosalyn S. Yalow, "A Physicist in Biomedical Investigation," *Physics Today,* 32 (October 1979), 25–29.

25. Norman R. F. Maier, *Principles of Human Relations* (New York: John Wiley, 1952), p. 172; see also Strauss and Sayles, *Personnel,* p. 186.

26. Theodore Sorenson, *Decision Making in the White House* (New York: Columbia University Press, 1963), pp. 22–42.

27. U.S. Congress, House, Committee on Appropriations, Subcommittee on Labor and Health, Education and Welfare, *Hearings, Department of Labor and Health, Education and Welfare Appropriations* 109th Cong., FY 1977, Part 6, pp. 37–38.

Chapter 3: Communication and Leadership

1. Ralph M. Stogdill, "Leadership, Membership and Organization," *Psychological Bulletin,* 47 (1950), 1–14.

2. Grover Starling, *Managing the Public Sector* (Homewood, Ill.: Dorsey Press, 1977), p. 346.

3. Harold Koontz and Cyril O'Donnell, *Essentials of Management,* 2d ed. (New York: McGraw-Hill, 1978), p. 439.

4. John R. Russell, *Cases in Urban Management* (Cambridge, Mass.: MIT Press, 1974), p. 266.

5. Koontz and O'Donnell, *Essentials of Management,* p. 439.

6. For a discussion of this literature and subsequent leadership

research, see Ralph M. Stogdill, *Handbook of Leadership* (New York: Free Press, 1974).

7. Kurt Lewin, Ronald Lippitt, and Ralph K. White, "Patterns of Aggressive Behavior in Experimentally Created 'Social Climates,'" *Journal of Social Psychology*, 10 (May 1939), 271–99.

8. See Rensis Likert, *New Patterns of Management* (New York: McGraw-Hill, 1961) and *The Human Organization* (New York: McGraw-Hill, 1967).

9. *The New Managerial Grid* (Houston, Tex.: Gulf Publishing Co., 1978).

10. Ibid., p. 217.

11. Robert Tannenbaum and Warren Schmidt, "How to Choose a Leadership Pattern," *Harvard Business Review*, 36 (March/April 1958), 95–101.

12. George Strauss and Leonard R. Sayles, *Personnel: The Human Problems of Management*, 3d ed. (Englewood Cliffs, N.J.: Prentice-Hall, 1972), p. 159.

13. Paul Hersey and Kenneth H. Blanchard, *Management of Organizational Behavior*, 2d ed. (Englewood Cliffs, N.J.: Prentice-Hall, 1972).

14. Abraham Maslow, *Motivation and Personality* (New York: Harper and Brothers, 1954).

15. Abraham Maslow, *The Farther Reaches of Human Nature* (New York: Viking, 1971), p. 43.

16. Fred E. Fiedler, *A Theory of Leadership Effectiveness* (New York: McGraw-Hill, 1967), p. 261.

17. The subject of blockages is discussed perceptively in Herbert Simon, Donald W. Smithburg, and Victor A. Thompson, "The Communication Process," *Public Administration: Concepts and Cases*, edited by Richard J. Stillman II (Boston: Houghton Mifflin, 1976), 117–83. Their work emphasizes the importance of understanding communication barriers and identifies a framework for studying blockages in public agencies.

Chapter 4: Language

1. See George E. Berkley, *The Craft of Public Administration* (Boston: Allyn and Bacon, 1975), p. 227.

2. Three excellent books on words and their meanings are: Samuel I. Hayakawa, *Language in Action* (New York: Harcourt, Brace and Co., 1941); Anatol Rapoport, *Science and the Goals of Man: A Study in Semantic Orientation* (New York: Harper and Row, 1950); and Geoffrey

Wagner, *On the Wisdom of Words* (Princeton, N.J.: D. Van Nostrand, 1968).

3. Volume 7, sec. 15.315.

4. The need to repeat must be balanced with limits on an employee's time and the general preference for short messages.

5. See Rudolf Flesch, *The Art of Readable Writing* (New York: Harper and Brothers, 1949) and *How to Test Readability* (New York: Harper and Brothers, 1951).

6. An adz is a heavy, curved tool for working with timber. Xaz is a musical notation in the Armenian church liturgy.

7. Industrial psychologists have used this formula to measure the readability of employee handbooks. See Keith Davis, "Readability Changes in Employee Handbooks of Identical Companies During a Fifteen-Year Period," *Personnel Psychology*, 21 (1968), 413–20.

8. Rapoport, *Science and the Goals of Man*, p. 42.

Chapter 5: Frame of Reference

1. George E. Berkley, *The Craft of Public Administration* (Boston: Allyn and Bacon, 1975), chapter 7.

2. Charles R. Wright, *Mass Communication* (New York: Random House, 1965); chapter 5 offers a review of research on how people screen communications.

3. Quoted in Seymour M. Hersh, "The Assault on Ky Chanh, South Vietnam," *Public Administration: Concepts and Cases*, edited by Richard J. Stillman II (Boston: Houghton Mifflin, 1976), pp. 185–91.

4. David Krech and Richard S. Crutchfield, "Perceiving the World," *The Process and Effects of Mass Communication*, edited by Wilbur Schramm (Urbana: University of Illinois Press, 1965), pp. 116–37, offers a good review of research on internal screening; as does Charles E. Osgood and Percy H. Tannenbaum, "Attitude Change and the Principle of Congruity," pp. 251–60, in the same volume. See also Terence Mitchell, *People in Organizations: Understanding Their Behavior* (New York: McGraw-Hill, 1978), pp. 93–101.

5. Mustafa Sherif, *The Psychology of Social Norms* (New York: Harper, 1936) describes experiments where subjects modified their estimates of objective phenomena (e.g., the distance a light moves, the length of a line) to conform with group estimates.

6. Patrick V. Murphy and Thomas Plate, *Commissioner: A View from the Top of American Law Enforcement* (New York: Simon and Schuster, 1977), p. 128.

7. Ibid.

8. Samuel Stouffer et al., "Barriers to Understanding Between Officers and Enlisted Men," *Reader in Bureaucracy*, edited by Robert K. Merton et al. (New York: Free Press, 1952), pp. 265–72. It might be interesting to do Stouffer's survey again and see if officer misperception has changed in the intervening time period.

9. Harold Koontz and Cyril O'Donnell, *Essentials of Management*, 2d ed. (New York: McGraw-Hill, 1978), p. 401.

10. Hersh, "The Assault on Ky Chahn, South Vietnam."

11. Chapter 13 examines specific techniques for conducting meetings.

12. Herbert Kaufman, *The Forest Ranger: A Study in Administrative Behavior* (Baltimore, Md.: Johns Hopkins Press, 1960), p. 186.

Chapter 6: Status Differences

1. Ken Auletta, "Profiles: Mayor Edward I. Koch—Part I," *New Yorker* (September 10, 1979), pp. 54–119.

2. Ibid., pp. 101–2.

3. Rufus E. Miles, Jr., "The Origin and Meaning of Miles' Law," *Public Administration Review*, 38 (September/October 1978), 399–403.

4. Anthony Downs, *Inside Bureaucracy* (Boston: Little, Brown, 1967), p. 110. Downs writes with great insight on the subject of status distortion in public agencies.

5. The concept of chain distortion appears in Gordon Tullock, *The Politics of Bureaucracy* (Washington, D.C.: Public Affairs Press, 1965), pp. 137–93.

6. Downs, *Inside Bureaucracy*, p. 123.

7. "Street-level" bureaucrats are those entry-level administrators who actually have contact with citizens seeking help from or being controlled by public agencies. The evocative term is used by Michael Lipsky in "Street-Level Bureaucracy and the Analysis of Urban Reform," *Urban Affairs Quarterly*, 6 (June 1971), 391–408, and *Street-Level Bureaucracy* (New York: Russell Sage Foundation, 1980).

8. Agency heads issue orders in so many areas that they lack time (and specialized expertise) to make each one specific.

9. Jonathan Daniels, *Frontier on the Potomac* (New York: Macmillan, 1946), pp. 31–32.

10. Downs, *Inside Bureaucracy*, p. 136.

11. John Anderson, "What's Blocking Upward Communication?" *Personnel Administration*, 31 (January/February 1968), 5–7, 19–20.

12. Thomas C. Clary, "Motivation through Positive Stroking," *Public Personnel Management* (March/April 1973), pp. 113–117.

13. Managers should always use items 1 through 3. The nature of the

problem, the communicator's background, and constraints of time, budget and previous commitments determine whether the manager can implement items 4 through 6.

14. Downs, *Inside Bureaucracy*, p. 120.

15. George Strauss and Leonard R. Sayles, *Personnel: The Human Problems of Management*, 3d ed. (Englewood Cliffs, N.J.: Prentice-Hall, 1972), p. 299.

16. For example, see Lyndall F. Urwick, "The Span of Control—Some Facts about the Fables," *Advanced Management*, 21 (November 1956), 5–15.

17. For example, see Harold Koontz, "Making Theory Operational: The Span of Management," *Journal of Management Studies* (October 1966), pp. 229–43.

18. John R. Russell, *Cases in Urban Management* (Cambridge, Mass.: MIT Press, 1974), p. 117.

19. Ibid., p. 116.

20. Miles, "Origin and Meaning of Miles' Law," p. 401.

21. Harry Hatry, R. E. Winnie, and D. M. Fiske, *Practical Program Evaluation for State and Local Government Officials* (Washington, D.C.: Urban Institute, 1973), p. 27.

22. Ibid.

23. For an analysis of big-city fire department reports see Hindy Lauer Schachter, "Open and Closed Municipal Bureaucracies: A Comparative Approach," Ph.D. dissertation, Columbia University, 1978.

24. Russell, *Cases in Urban Management*, p. 378. Some workers admit they do this, but it is impossible to gauge how widespread the problem is.

25. Downs, *Inside Bureaucracy*, p. 147.

26. See the discussion in Frederick C. Thayer, "Values, Truth and Administration: God or Mammon?" *Public Administration Review*, 40 (January/February 1980), 91–98.

Chapter 7: Geographical Distance

1. Daniel Elazar, *American Federalism: A View from the States* (New York: Crowell, 1972).

2. The importance of a field administrator's responding to the desires of local communities is associated with the "new" public administration of the 1960s and the movement to decentralize big-city agencies. See, for example, Frank Marini (ed.), *Towards a New Public Administration: The Minnowbrook Perspective* (Scranton, Penn.: Chandler, 1971), and

Dwight Waldo (ed.), *Public Administration in a Time of Turbulence* (Scranton, Penn.: Chandler, 1971).

3. Ronald Randall, "Presidential Power versus Bureaucratic Intransigence: The Influence of the Nixon Administration on Welfare Policy," *American Political Science Review*, 73 (September 1979), 795–810.

4. Jong Jun, "Management by Objectives in Government: Theory and Practice," *Sage Professional Papers in Administrative and Policy Studies*, 3 (1976), 3–30.

5. Gifford Pinchot, *Breaking New Ground* (New York: Harcourt, Brace, 1947), p. 162.

6. Herbert A. Simon, Donald Smithburg, and Victor A. Thompson, "The Communication Process," *Public Administration: Concepts and Cases*, edited by Richard J. Stillman II (Boston: Houghton Mifflin, 1976), pp. 117–83.

7. Ibid. The authors discuss the problem in terms of housing regulations.

8. Joseph Massie, *Essentials of Management*, 2d ed. (Englewood Cliffs, N.J.: Prentice-Hall, 1971), p. 97.

9. Kenneth L. Kraemer and James Perry, "The Federal Push to Bring Computer Applications to Local Government," *Public Administration Review*, 39 (May/June 1979), 260–70.

10. Robert Buchele, *The Management of Business and Public Organizations* (New York: McGraw-Hill, 1977), p. 251.

11. Ibid., p. 244, analyzes division of responsibility between program managers and EDP specialists.

12. See, for example, Kenneth L. Kraemer, "The Evolution of Information Systems for Urban Administrators," *Public Administration Review*, 29 (July/August 1969), 389–98, and Gilbert Fairholm, "A Reality Basis for Management Information System Decisions," *Public Administration Review*, 39 (March/April 1979), 176–79.

13. See, for example, James Q. Wilson, "The Bureaucracy Problem," *Public Interest*, 6 (Winter 1967), 3–9. The perennial tension between pressures for centralization and decentralization is analyzed in Herbert Kaufman, "Administrative Decentralization and Political Power," *Public Administration Review*, 29 (January/February 1969), 3–14.

Chapter 8: Time Limits

1. See C. Northcote Parkinson, *Parkinson's Law and Other Studies in Administration* (Boston: Houghton Mifflin, 1957), p. 2.

2. Quoted in Bruce Adams, "The Limitations of Muddling Through:

Does Anyone in Washington Really Think Anymore?" *Public Administration Review*, 39 (November/December 1979), p. 548.

   3. Ibid., p. 546.

   4. Anthony Downs, *Inside Bureaucracy* (Boston: Little, Brown, 1967), p. 183.

   5. Adams, "Limitations of Muddling Through," p. 546.

   6. Ibid., p. 551.

   7. Ibid.

   8. Related in Grover Starling, *Managing the Public Sector* (Homewood, Ill.: Dorsey Press, 1977), p. 2.

   9. R. Alec MacKenzie, *Managing Time at the Top* (New York: The Presidents Association, 1970).

   10. Parkinson, *Parkinson's Law*, p. 24.

Chapter 9: Communicating Orally: How and What to Say

   1. John P. Moncur and Harrison M. Karr, *Developing Your Speaking Voice*, 2d ed. (New York: Harper and Row, 1972).

   2. See, for example, W. A. Mambert, *Presenting Technical Ideas: A Guide to Audience Communication* (New York: John Wiley and Sons, 1968), p. 148.

   3. Arnold E. Schneider, William C. Donaghy, and Pamela Jane Newman, *Organizational Communication* (New York: McGraw-Hill, 1975), pp. 96–97.

   4. Carl Hovland, Arthur Lumsdaine, and Fred Sheffield, "The Effect of Presenting 'One Side' versus 'Both Sides' in Changing Opinions on a Controversial Subject," *The Process and Effects of Mass Communication*, edited by Wilbur Schramm (Urbana: University of Illinois Press, 1965), pp. 261–74.

Chapter 10: Training

   1. James N. Mosel, "How to Feed Back Performance Results to Trainees," *People in Public Service: A Reader in Public Personnel Administration*, edited by Robert T. Golembiewski and Michael Cohen (Itasca, Ill.: Peacock, 1976), pp. 389–97.

   2. An "adequate" response is clear and concise. In most situations, managers can ask "Is that clearer?" or "Did I answer your point?" and enlarge their explanations if the answer is "No."

   3. See the distinction between "following" and "producing" a pattern in Jonas Soltis, *An Introduction to the Analysis of Educational Concepts* (Reading, Mass.: Addison-Wesley, 1968), pp. 47–9.

   4. See, for example, Earl Gomersall and M. Scott Myers,

"Break-Through in On-the-Job Training," *Harvard Business Review*, 44 (July/August 1966), 62-72.

5. Most definitions of "management" stress the manager's role coordinating and directing the work of other people. See, for example, Harold Koontz and Cyril O'Donnell, *Essentials of Management*, 2d ed. (New York: McGraw-Hill, 1978), p. 4.

6. See, for example, George Odiorne, *Management by Objectives: A System of Managerial Leadership* (New York: Pitman, 1965) and "MBO in State Government," *Public Adminstration Review*, 36 (January/February 1976), 28-33.

7. Henry L. Tosi, John R. Rizzo, and Stephen J. Carroll, "Setting Goals in Management by Objectives," *California Management Review*, 12 (1970), 70-8.

8. MBO works best when the manager can quantify objectives. It is easy to write an objective to eliminate ineligibles from the welfare rolls but harder to write one concerning responsive care for those who are eligible. Agencies using MBO have to pay special attention that they do not stress quantifiable goals at the expense of other, equally important attainments.

9. See, for example, Alva Kindall and James Gatza, "Positive Program for Performance Appraisal," *Harvard Business Review*, 41 (November/December 1963), 153-60.

Chapter 11: Interviews

1. F. J. Roethlisberger and W. J. Dickson, *Management and the Worker* (Cambridge, Mass.: Harvard University Press, 1939).

2. See, for example, Carl R. Rogers and F. J. Roethlisberger, "Barriers and Gateways to Communication," *Harvard Business Review*, 30 (July/August 1952), 46-52.

3. W. Richard Scott, "Professional Employees in a Bureaucratic Structure: Social Work," *The Semi-Professions and Their Organization*, edited by Amitai Etzioni (New York: Free Press, 1969), pp. 82-140.

4. *The Appraisal Interview* (New York: John Wiley and Sons, 1958).

5. Harold J. Leavitt, *Management* (Chicago: University of Chicago Press, 1964), p. 129.

6. See, for example, Paul Strauss, "The Rating Game," *Personnel Administration*, 32 (January/February 1969), 44-47.

Chapter 12: Grievances

1. The states are: Alaska, California, Connecticut, Delaware, Florida, Georgia, Hawaii, Idaho, Indiana, Iowa, Kansas, Kentucky, Maine, Maryland, Massachusetts, Michigan, Minnesota, Missouri,

Montana, Nebraska, New Hampshire, New Jersey, New York, North Dakota, Oklahoma, Oregon, Pennsylvania, Rhode Island, South Dakota, Texas, Vermont, Washington, Wisconsin, and Wyoming. See Stephen L. Hayford, "Local Government Residency Requirements and Labor Relations: Implications and Choices for Public Administrators," *Public Administration Review*, 38 (September/October 1978), 482–86.

2. "Federal Employee Ranks at All-Time High," *Public Administration Times* (June 15, 1979), 8.

3. Jack Stieber, "State, Local Unions Pass Industry and Still Going," *LMRS Newsletter*, 2 (July 1971), 1, as cited by Felix A. Nigro, "The Implications of Collective Bargaining for Public Administration," *Public Administration Review*, 32 (March/April 1972), 120–26.

4. "Federal Employee Ranks at All-Time High."

5. Anthony Russo, "Management's View of the New York City Experience," *Unionization of Municipal Employees*, edited by Robert H. Connery and William V. Farr (New York: Academy of Political Science, 1971), pp. 87–8.

6. Hindy Lauer Schachter, "Collective Bargaining and School Policy," *Peabody Journal of Education*, 58 (October 1980), 39–44.

7. See, for example, David T. Stanley with the assistance of Carole L. Cooper, *Managing Local Government under Union Pressure* (Washington, D.C.: Brookings Institute, 1972) and Sterling D. Spero and John M. Capozzola, *The Urban Community and Its Unionized Bureaucracies* (New York: Dunellen, 1973).

8. Irvin Molotsky, "Education Boards See Levittown as a Model for Resisting Strikes," *New York Times* (November 20, 1978), A1.

9. Nigro, "Implications of Collective Bargaining."

10. Unions include grievance procedures in contracts to ensure that management treats complaints in a fair and equitable way.

11. In 1968, New York City's United Federation of Teachers staged a three-month strike over a grievance concerning the involuntary transfer of nineteen teachers.

12. "Article XI—Hours and Schedules, Section 5," *Agreement between District Council 37, A.F.S.C.M.E., AFL-CIO and the City of New York and the New York City Health and Hospitals Corporation, January 1, 1976–June 30, 1978*, p. 80.

13. Robert B. McKersie, "Avoiding Written Grievances by Problem-Solving: An Outside View," *Personnel Psychology*, 17 (Winter 1964), 367–79.

14. *Agreement between District Council 37 and New York City*, pp. 51–2.

15. Ibid., p. 52.

16. As a condition for invoking arbitration, the employee and the union waive their rights to submit the dispute to any other administrative or judicial tribunal. Contracts generally stipulate which grievances go to arbitration; an agreement may exclude certain issues. For these disputes, the grievance process ends at Step III.

17. Francis Ferris, "Contract Interpretation—A Bread-and-Butter Talent," *Public Personnel Management*, 4 (July/August 1975), 223–30.

18. Paul Prasow, *Arbitration and Collective Bargaining* (New York: McGraw-Hill, 1970), p. 51.

Chapter 13: Staff Meetings

1. R. Alex Mackenzie, *The Time Trap* (New York: AMACOM, 1972), pp. 103–4.

2. Sometimes managers have little choice about whom to invite; they must include all people with a certain status. This analysis pertains to those situations where the leader plans the roster.

3. Ken Auletta, "Profiles: Mayor Edward I. Koch," *New Yorker* (September 10, 1979), 54–119.

4. Ibid., p. 96.

5. John R. Russell, *Cases in Urban Management* (Cambridge, Mass.: MIT Press, 1974), p. 508.

6. Alex F. Osborn, *Applied Imagination* (New York: Charles Scribner's Sons, 1957), pp. 84, 228.

7. John Morgan, *Practical Guide to Conference Leadership* (New York: McGraw-Hill, 1966), pp. 153–54.

8. Arnold E. Schneider, William C. Donaghy, and Pamela Jane Newman, *Organizational Communication* (New York: McGraw-Hill, 1975), pp. 160–61.

9. Strategies for constructing and presenting effective audiovisuals are offered in W. A. Mambert, *Presenting Technical Ideas* (New York: John Wiley, 1968), Chap. 9.

10. Gerald F. Wheeler and Larry D. Kirkpatrick, "Eclipse '79: Physicists Go Public," *Physics Teacher*, 17 (October 1979), 443–48.

11. A good source for these films is the Reuben Donnelly Corporation in New York City.

Chapter 14: Collecting and Organizing Information

1. Martin Smith, *I Hate to See a Manager Cry* (Reading, Mass.: Addison-Wesley, 1973), p. 26.

2. Carl Swidorski, "Sample Surveys: Help for the 'Out-of-House'

Evaluator," *Public Administration Review*, 40 (January/February 1980), 67-71.

3. The need to offer social support is identified in Gregory A. Daneke and Patricia Kolbus-Edwards, "Survey Research for Public Administrators," *Public Administration Review*, 39 (September/October 1979), 421-26.

4. Ibid.

5. A well-written, reliable guide to sampling for people with little background in statistics is Morris Slonim, *Sampling* (New York: Simon and Schuster, 1960).

6. These topics are only a few from a several-page list of public administration bibliographies available from Vance Bibliographies, P.O. Box 229, Monticello, Illinois 61856.

7. Published by the American Society for Public Administration, 1120 G St., N.W., Washington, D.C. 20036.

Chapter 15: Presenting Information: Content and Style

1. Since internal agency memoranda are not protected by the Freedom of Information Act, managers may refuse to give you any. You should seek them either in an agency where you work or where family or friends work.

2. Joseph P. Viteritti, "New York's Management Plan and Reporting System: A Descriptive Analysis," *Public Administration Review*, 38 (July/August 1978), 376-81.

3. Ken Auletta, "Profiles: Mayor Edward I. Koch," *New Yorker* (September 10, 1979), 54-119.

4. Ralph E. Thayer, "The Local Government Annual Report as a Policy Planning Opportunity," *Public Administration Review*, 38 (July/August 1978), 373-76.

Chapter 16: Presenting Statistical Information

1. Lewis Carroll, *Alice in Wonderland* (New York: New American Library, 1960), p. 62.

GLOSSARY

Audience: listeners or readers. Effective communications take into account the background, tastes, knowledge, and values of the intended audience.

Channels: the means for transmitting information, e.g., interviews, books, papers, reports.

Communication: information exchange; a process requiring a communicator, information, channels, and an audience.

Communicator: the person initiating information exchange; the one who transmits information.

Congruent: in accord, coinciding. Effective communicators make certain that their message is congruent with the educational level and interests of the intended audience.

Content: a communication's topic or substantive information. Every message has both style and content.

Face-to-face: oral communication where initiator and audience interact. Face-to-face permits an exchange of ideas, allowing initiators to modify their approach and make the message easier for the audience to understand.

Feedback: knowledge of the results of behavior from those directly affected. Feedback enables the initiator of a communication to recognize his impact on the audience and to modify his approach accordingly.

Flowchart: diagram that depicts in chronological sequence the essential steps in an agency process. Flowcharts identify alternative actions that are available at each stage along with the consequences of each (in process terms).

Goal: broad purpose; the reason for a given action or communication.

Options paper: a paper analyzing alternative policies, plans, or processes which a public agency can pursue. The writer identifies arguments for and against pursuing each alternative.

Position paper: a paper advocating a particular course of action from what may be a wide range of plausible alternatives. The writer delineates arguments in support of the given public policy or plan.

Progress report: a report describing an ongoing set of activities in a public agency. The writer identifies the purpose of activities, accomplishments to date, problems encountered, solutions tried, and the need (if any) to revise plans.

Public agency: an organization within the executive branch of federal, state, or local government mandated by the legislature to implement certain public programs. Every agency has a broad purpose (or goal) which it tries to accomplish. The *best* agency communication system is the one that brings the organization closest to achieving its goal.

Selective exposure: a process whereby people read or listen to communications that reinforce their views and ignore all others.

Selective perception: a process whereby people distort the meaning of what they see and hear to make it consistent with their own beliefs.

Selective retention: a process whereby people remember messages that they agree with and forget those that are unpleasant, confusing, or unclear.

Strategy: a way of achieving a goal. First know where you want to go, then design appropriate methods for getting there.

Style: the format and tone of a communication; the way the topic or information is presented. Every communication has both style and content.

Summary: an abridgement of a written or oral presentation. In one page or less, the writer identifies major points without adding any information not contained in the original message.

INDEX